JEAN LIPMAN

AMERICAN FOLK ART

IN WOOD, METAL AND STONE

183 ILLUSTRATIONS
FOUR COLOR PLATES

DOVER PUBLICATIONS, INC.
NEW YORK

Published in Canada by General Publishing
Company, Ltd., 30 Lesmill Road, Don Mills,
Toronto, Ontario.
Published in the United Kingdom by Constable
and Company, Ltd., 10 Orange Street, London WC 2.

This Dover edition, first published in 1972, is an
unabridged republication of the work originally
published by Pantheon Books, Inc., New York,
in 1948.

International Standard Book Number: 0-486-22816-9
Library of Congress Catalog Card Number: 75-184123

Manufactured in the United States of America
Dover Publications, Inc.
180 Varick Street
New York, N. Y. 10014

DEDICATED TO THE INDEX OF AMERICAN DESIGN
WITH THE HOPE THAT ITS PIONEER WORK
OF RECORDING AMERICAN FOLK ART
WILL BE ACTIVELY CONTINUED

ACKNOWLEDGMENTS

This book is most largely indebted to the Index of American Design, National Gallery of Art, whose files of annotated renderings and photographs of folk sculpture were the cornerstone of this study and whose original photographs and renderings in color were made available for reproduction. I take the opportunity to express my appreciation for the generous cooperation on the part of Erwin O. Christensen, Curator of the Index, and Ann Watkins, assistant to the Curator.

I also wish to thank all the other institutions and individuals who made available photographs here reproduced and provided all sorts of information—with special gratitude for the assistance of the Museum of Modern Art, the Newark Museum, Colonial Williamsburg, Inc., the Mariners' Museum, the Bucks County Historical Society, the Downtown Gallery, the Insurance Company of North America, the Cigar Institute of America; the American Antiquarian Society for a number of photographs of gravestone portraits, given to the Society by Harriette M. Forbes and first published in her *Gravestones of Early New England;* Samuel M. Green, who most generously allowed me to touch upon the content of his unpublished manuscript on Edbury Hatch; Pauline A. Pinckney, who loaned several photographs which were published in her *American Figureheads and Their Carvers;* the Narragansett Brewing Company who provided the color frontispiece; also Harriette M. Forbes, Robert S. Kuhn, Joel Barber, Anthony W. Pendergast, Heathcote M. Woolsey, Carl W. Drepperd, Holger Cahill, Lucius Beebe, Titus C. Geesey, and William L. Warren.

I am greatly indebted to Edith Gregor Halpert who read the book in manuscript and made many valuable suggestions, and to Howard Lipman who helped and advised me from plans through proofs. I wish to acknowledge the kind permission of Joel Barber to quote an anecdote from *Wild Fowl Decoys* and to reproduce two drawings of decoys from this book; of the Vanguard Press to quote the gravestone epitaphs from E. V. Mitchell's *It's an Old New England Custom;* of *Old-Time New England* to reproduce the early weathervane patterns published in its issue for October, 1940.

I want, finally, to call attention to my large indebtedness to a few catalogues and books: the Newark Museum exhibition catalogue, *American Folk Sculpture,* and the Museum of Modern Art exhibition catalogue, *American Folk Art,* from which portions of Holger Cahill's discussions of folk art have been quoted in the Foreword, with his permission and that of the two museums (the third paragraph is quoted from the Museum of Modern Art catalogue, the rest from the Newark Museum catalogue); also the Williamsburg collection catalogue, *American Folk Art* by Edith Gregor Halpert, Pauline A. Pinckney's *American Figureheads and Their Carvers,* and Joel Barber's *Wild Fowl Decoys.*

CONTENTS

LIST OF ILLUSTRATIONS

The information on ownership dates from 1948. Most of the author's personal collection is now in the New York State Historical Association, Cooperstown. The Philadelphia Museum of Art now owns most of the Titus C. Geesey Collection, and many of the decoys collected by Joel Barber are at the Shelburne Museum.

WEATHERVANES

CIGAR-STORE FIGURES AND OTHER TRADE SIGNS

CIRCUS AND CARROUSEL CARVINGS

TOYS

FOREWORD

American folk sculpture was first brought to the attention of the general public through two large exhibitions of folk art at the Newark Museum in 1931 and at the Museum of Modern Art in 1932. Holger Cahill's prefaces to these two exhibition catalogues are definitive essays that sum up the basic character and special quality of the native American sculptures which are presented in this book. The excerpts which follow are reprinted with his permission:

These sculptures were made by anonymous craftsmen and amateurs, carvers, carpenters, cabinet-makers, shipwrights, blacksmiths, stonecutters, metal workers, sailors, farmers and laborers. The work of these men . . . is folk art in its truest sense—it is an expression of the common people and not an expression of a small cultured class. Folk art usually has not much to do with the fashionable art of its period. It is never the product of art movements, but comes out of craft traditions, plus that personal something of the rare craftsman who is an artist by nature if not by training. This art is based not on measurements or calculations but on feeling, and it rarely fits in with the standards of realism. It goes straight to the fundamentals of art—rhythm, design, balance, proportion, which the folk artist feels instinctively. . .

[It] has significance for us as a genuine expression of the art spirit of the American people, and as a demonstration of the fact that talent has never been lacking in America even when opportunities for the study of art techniques have been very limited. There is a remarkable variety of personal styles in these carvings and castings, and a great deal of vigor and inventiveness even when the technique is crude and primitive. It is among objects such as these that we must look for the earliest American sculpture, and among their makers we may discover sculptural talent of a high order.

There is no doubt that these works have many technical deficiencies from the academic and naturalistic point of view, but with the artists who made them realism was a passion and not merely a technique. Surface realism meant nothing to them. It might be contended that this results from a lack of technical proficiency. The actual reason appears to be that the folk artists tried to set down not so much what they saw as what they knew and what they felt. Their art mirrors the sense and the sentiment of a community, and is an authentic expression of American experience.

Until very recently American folk sculpture has been almost without honor in its own country. Contemporary interest in it began with the modern artists who found in this folk expression a kinship with their own work, and a proof that there is an American tradition in the arts which is as old as the European colonization of this country, and which is vital today. A number of artists and collectors have been gathering this material for some years, not because it is naive, or quaint, or crude, or because of its historical associations, but because it has genuine sculptural quality, and because they see in it an evidence of the enduring vitality of the American tradition.

The story of American folk sculpture would make one of the most fascinating chapters in the history of the arts of design in the United States. When this folk art is better known, it will do much toward giving us a better perspective of American art history, and toward creating greater respect for the American tradition in the arts.

SHIP FIGUREHEADS AND ORNAMENTS

IN BYGONE DAYS a ship was almost a human individual in the eyes of the crew, and the ship's name and her figurehead personified the special character of the ship. Centuries of tradition lay behind the seaman's feeling of superstition and awe for the figurehead. The Greeks and Romans had placed carved images of their gods on the galleys to placate those gods, and the figureheads of the ancient Norse warships were designed to strike terror into the enemy and scare away their guardian spirits. During the Renaissance in Europe and the following centuries in England the lavish carvings that ornamented the ships bore witness to the wealth and strength of the nations that launched them. In early America the figureheads and ornamental carvings were equally representative of the success and triumph of Yankee ships. Each of these vessels played a part in building the great new nation, and the figurehead symbolized the living spirit of the ship. Romantic in conception, it also suggested something of the hidden poetry in the sea captain's nature, and the crew's composite sense of the romance of seafaring.

Joseph Conrad makes dramatically clear in his story, *A Smile of Fortune,* that the figurehead was looked upon in a very personal way by the captain and was associated in his mind with the luck of his ship and his own fortunes. Injury to or loss of the original figurehead was considered an especially ill omen. In Conrad's tale the ship's figurehead had been lost and a suggestion was made that a new one could be secured, for one happened to be available at a shipyard at that moment. The disheartened captain of the headless ship flushed red as if something improper had been suggested, said he would as soon think of getting a new wife, and asked whether he seemed "the sort that would pick up with another man's cast-off figurehead?" It is interesting to find in an old newspaper account that when the figurehead was removed from the ship *Centennial* an old sailor protested, "It is enough to blanch the faces of old seamen to sail without a figurehead."

There have been accounts recording the strange fact that some of the American figureheads, falling into the hands of South Seas chiefs on trading voyages, were set up and worshiped as idols. No wonder then that a ship's own crew felt a superstitious attachment to their figurehead, and often carried fragments of wood sliced from it in their pockets to bring them luck on a voyage. That American sailors endowed these mascot figures with supernatural qualities is indicated by the amusing history of a binnacle figure made in New York in 1851 for the clipper ship *N. B. Palmer* (Fig. 14). This little wooden tar made just one trip to China for tea. He was then removed because the sailors claimed that the eyes of the figure would move at night and distract their attention from the compass.

The attitudes of the skipper, the shipowner, and even the ordinary seaman all played some part in the ship carver's approach to his trade. He was used to carry on his work in a shop or sail loft near the shipyard and so he was not only schooled in the knowledge of shipbuilding, but directly acquainted with the ships he was to ornament and steeped in the traditions of the sea.

Each ship required a different kind of carved decoration, which was designed to suit the individual ideas of its builder and owner, and which was adapted to its basic structure and function. For the prow of a New Bedford whaler the carver made a sturdy portrait of the shipowner's wife or daughter looking out to sea; a slender white-and-gold maiden with windswept drapery heralded the return of a majestic clipper as she entered her Salem port laden with spices and tea and silks from the Orient; a fierce eagle flew from the bow of a frigate built to sail for the United States Navy; a portrait of the President stood stiffly at the bow of a handsome new steamboat. When we look today at these weatherbeaten figures jutting out from museum walls it is important to try to visualize them, freshly painted, as they traveled the high seas at the heads of their ships.

In order to simplify our discussion we will limit it to a few major types of American ship decorations. The early Navy and merchant vessels were generally adorned with figureheads and their sterns and quarter galleries were elaborately carved. During the eighteenth century both technique and subject matter reflected English traditions, and it was not until the nineteenth century that an original style was developed. William Rush of Philadelphia executed prow and stern decorations for many of the early ships, and has become popularly known as our first native sculptor. His work does not, however, in any way typify the native carving —the subject of this book—which was produced by men who considered themselves artisans and craftsmen and never aspired to the title of sculptor. Rush was apprenticed at an early age to a ship carver from London, and as a prominent member of the Academy of Fine Arts he worked all his life in an English-style, academic tradition. As a sculptor his work might be paralleled with that of Benjamin West in the field of painting, and his œuvre is at the opposite pole of the native tradition that we wish to illustrate here.

The figurehead of Andrew Jackson (Fig. 12), made in 1834 for the *Constitution* by Laban S. Beecher, a Boston carver, is typical of the robust Yankee craft that had developed into a vigorous folk art during the nineteenth century. The *Constitution,* from the time of her building in 1797, was regarded by the people as a symbol of American naval power, and the choice of her third figurehead became a national issue. "Old Ironsides'" figurehead of Andrew Jackson, dressed in plain clothes, holding his hat and cane in one hand and a scroll of the Constitution in the other, still seems to symbolize the tough endurance and simple dignity of our young nation, as personified by "Old Hickory."

The huge eagle carved by John H. Bellamy of Portsmouth, New Hampshire, was one of the last great figureheads for a Navy ship (Fig. 20). It was made for the steam frigate *Lancaster* when she was reconditioned at the Portsmouth Navy Yard in 1880, and Bellamy worked at his carving in a part of the mold loft on the second floor of an old granite building next to the dock. When the great eagle was finished it measured over eighteen feet from one wing tip to the other. It heralded its ship in all the foreign seas where the *Lancaster* continued her valiant career, and

it gloriously represents the old Navy still as it spreads its wings in the confines of
the Mariners' Museum at Newport News.

The whale ships, relatively small, built deep and strong to carry a heavy load,
were devoted to hard work on long, strenuous voyages. Their small size and strictly
utilitarian structure partly explains why carved decoration was kept to a minimum
and the figureheads were small and plain. As much to the point, in accounting for
the homely character of whale-ship carvings, is the fact that old New Bedford and

1. Alice Knowles

Nantucket, the chief whaling ports, were dominated by the Quakers with their dis-
like of luxury and show. The story has often been told of the fate of the elegant
female figure that was carved for the eighteenth-century whale ship *Rebecca* of
New Bedford—the Society of Friends disapproved of such extravagance and the
Quaker shipowner felt obliged to remove the head, which was buried in the sand
at the shore. A generation later the ship *Rousseau,* built in Philadelphia, was re-
modeled in New Bedford as a whaler under the direction of the shipowner George
Howland who had bought her. At that time the fine bust of Rousseau, carved by
Rush, was removed and replaced with a simple billethead.

The figureheads and stern carvings made for the whalers are perhaps the most
interesting of all as folk sculpture. Warships were most typically decorated with

figures of naval heroes and statesmen, clippers with beautiful maidens or Indian princesses, steamboats with important personages or American emblems. The frugal owner of a whale ship, when he ordered a figurehead, would most likely request a simple likeness of his or the captain's wife or daughter in her Sunday best. These unpretentious seagoing portraits seem peculiarly appropriate for the plain, stocky whalers, whose routine daily work was hard and dirty. Doubtless the Nantucket captain and his crew often longed for their trig island homes, with the smell of pies baking in the kitchen and the sight of sheep roaming the moors. It must have seemed to them that they took a bit of the spirit of home with them when their ship was named after the captain's wife—simply *Nancy*, *Polly*, or *Hannah*—and carried at the prow her buxom image as she appeared in everyday dress at home in her parlor or kitchen.

Typical figureheads preserved from old whalers are simple and natural in pose, expression and dress. "Alice Knowles" seen here on the whaler named after her is wearing high black boots and an ordinary country dress (Fig. 1). A bust figurehead of a neatly dressed young woman named Sally from the eighteenth-century whaler of Nantucket that bore her name, now the property of the State Street Trust Company in Boston, is one of the plainest Colonial portraits to be found. A sternboard carving from the *Eunice H. Adams* (Fig. 22), a whaling brig of Nantucket and then of New Bedford, is a forthright, serene portrait of a woman of one of the old New England whaling families. One can imagine that she is about to put down her book, look to her chowder in the summer kitchen, and then climb to the Walk to watch for the distant sails that would announce the return of a long-absent whale ship.

The famous mid-century clippers, designed for speed, were long, slender ships. Their figureheads, which leaned buoyantly out over the water, heads thrown back and hair and clothes blown as if facing a brisk wind, were the most glamorous of American carvings. At the time of the gold rush a number of experienced marine architects were becoming prominent as builders of the clipper ships that sped hordes of passengers to the coast. These men conceived the figurehead as an integral part of ship design, and so the carved figure became a structural extension of the long, converging lines of the prow. Now in a more horizontal position as it stood on a scroll which merged into the cutwater, the figurehead was simply carved and painted to harmonize with the clean, sleek lines of the clipper. Busts, eagles and conventional billets were used, but the full figure was the most popular and the most striking. Among the subjects of the clipper-ship figureheads were Indian maids and chiefs, allegorical figures, characters from literature and the stage, contemporary men and women, portraits of soldiers and statesmen. These figures all seem more flexible and graceful than those that decorated the whalers; they stood lightly poised or strode swiftly along with the same ease with which the ship they headed cut through the waves. The goddess from the *Glory of the Seas,* which now adorns the stairs of India House in New York and the Indian chief from the ship *Sachem* (Fig. 15) are typical examples. Longfellow, in his poem *The Building of the Ship,* writes of a clipper's figurehead with its carved white robes that seem to flutter in the wind. He describes the figure, appearing to pilot the ship as it glides along,

Guiding the vessel, in its flight,
By a path none other knows aright!

The age of steam brought a radical change of style to ship carving, for with the designing of steam vessels the projecting prow and its coordinated figurehead lost their function. Pilot-house eagles, paddle-box decorations and erect figureheads replaced the old carvings of stern and prow, and emphasis was shifted to minor inboard decoration. The most striking change was in the style of the figurehead, which became as static as the cigar-store figures which many of the carvers, with diminishing ship commissions, now began to execute.

The earlier ships had seldom displayed interesting interior decoration such as the carved eagle and snake (Fig. 21) originally placed over a cabin door. There was, however, a good deal of richly carved woodwork designed for the late steamers, and Bellamy carved scores of flat eagles finished with incised decoration and red, white, and blue paint, which were mounted over the doorways of cabins and of houses as well. These ornaments have been reproduced by the hundred, and after being left out to weather for a season have been sold in antique shops all over New England as "Bellamy eagles."

The Yankee craftsmen who were responsible for the fine native tradition of ship carving in America are too numerous to list. Pauline Pinckney appends to the text of her authoritative book on American figureheads, to which this brief introduction to the subject is largely indebted, the names of more than eight hundred carvers assembled from directories, newspapers, Navy records, and family papers. Only a few of the most outstanding carvers can be mentioned here. As the ship carvers also engaged in other types of carving and metal sculpture, some of their names will appear in connection with the making of weathervanes, trade signs, toys, and ornamental sculpture of various kinds.

"Deacon" Shem Drowne of Boston, whose weathervanes are illustrated in the next chapter, was also one of the earliest figurehead carvers, immortalized in Hawthorne's folk tale of *Drowne's Wooden Image*.

Samuel McIntire, renowned for his architectural carving, was the son of a carpenter and was trained in the Salem shipyards in the latter part of the eighteenth century. He executed a great deal of inboard and stern carving, for which numerous bills exist; and though he presumably carved a number of figureheads as well, the only one found to date which can certainly be attributed to him is the dainty lady holding a medallion portrait of Jefferson, reproduced as Fig. 5. Although this little figure, just thirty inches high, has always been considered a figurehead, it seems more likely to this author that it was a model carved by McIntire for full-scale execution in his shop.

Laban Beecher, previously mentioned as the carver of the *Constitution's* figurehead, and the Skillins of Boston were among the noteworthy eighteenth-century ship carvers. Simeon Skillin, whose portrait bust of Milton is reproduced in Fig. 180, was chiefly occupied with the carving of ship decoration and figureheads. Cooperation between ship carvers was very close, and we find that the Skillins were associated at one time with the Dodges, another family of carvers, and that Charles Dodge in turn worked with his contemporary John Mason.

Isaac Fowle and his sons were another outstanding family of Boston ship carvers, and the beautiful figurehead reproduced as Fig. 8, carved by Isaac Fowle about 1820, stood in front of the Boston shop to advertise this firm.

The Gleasons must be mentioned as another famous family of carvers who executed many fine figureheads for clipper ships.

The firm of Joseph Wilson & Son of Newburyport was primarily known for ship carvings, but also attracted public interest with the figures of famous men executed for Lord Timothy Dexter which are discussed in another chapter.

2. Ship *Wanderer*

We have mentioned John Bellamy who was for many years attached to the Portsmouth Navy Yard in New Hampshire. He also maintained private workshops in Portsmouth and across the river at Kittery, Maine, where he worked in a mold loft facing Pepperel Cove. He is known today as a carver of decorative eagles, but his Portsmouth business card indicates that he was a versatile carver indeed:

John H. Bellamy, figure and ornamental carver
Particular attention paid to house, ship, furniture,
sign and frame carving and garden figures.
No. 17 Daniel St., Portsmouth, N. H.

Charles A. L. Sampson of Bath, Maine, was another prolific carver who was an active maker of figureheads in the second half of the nineteenth century. One of his masterpieces is the figurehead from the *Belle of Bath*, a lady elegantly dressed in the fashion of the day for which the captain's daughter served as model

(Fig. 7). She seems to gaze across the ocean to some far-off destination for her ship, perhaps the Columbia River, or Hong Kong. The scrollwork on which she stands harmonizes perfectly with the rich scalloped design of her dress, and both echo in stylized form the rolling waves of the sea.

One of the carvers for the later whale ships was Henry J. Purrington of Mattapoiset, a Massachusetts town proud of its record of building fine whaling ships. Like his father and grandfather he was trained as a carpenter and he then turned to ship carving (see Fig. 2), being called "Henry Carver" to distinguish him from the older Purringtons.

Early carvers' shop signs, United States Navy drafts, customs house entry descriptions, advertisements and bills, and contemporary accounts of all kinds enable us to reconstruct the trade of ship carving as these men practiced it—the tools and materials they used, and their methods of designing, carving and painting.

Nearly every coast town along the Atlantic seaboard had a thriving shipyard. It was in these towns that the carvers maintained their shops and hung out their signs, and the local newspapers carried their advertisements. The craft of ship carving was carried on through an apprentice system, and we find carvers issuing certificates stating the length of time that an apprentice had worked and his qualifications as a carver. Old sketchbooks exist to show that carvers made preliminary sketches of their work to submit to the shipbuilders. It is told that the builder sometimes had the lines of the ship's head and the rake of the bow chalked on the floor of the carver's shop and the carver in turn completed the sketches with chalked figurehead designs to show the builder. It is known that figureheads were often made from sketches of living models or from models who actually posed for a carved portrait. The cutting of the figurehead was done mostly with large and small chisels, sets of which have been preserved. The figurehead and its scroll were generally carved of a single block, with arms and other projecting pieces fastened on separately. The figures were ordinarily polychromed "to life" but for the clipper ships they were often painted white with bits of gold leaf applied on ornamental details, to sparkle in the sun.

American ship carving, unlike most of the contemporary portrait and figure sculpture of the time, was relatively underivative, a fresh and vigorous product of the native tradition in American art. The figureheads preserved as relics of our earliest native sculpture communicate to our generation a vivid sense of the American past, with the tang of the old wharves of Commercial Street in Boston and Front Street in Philadelphia, of Salem and New Bedford and Nantucket.

During the hundred-odd years from about 1775 to the late nineteenth century there was developed in America a specifically native type of ship carving, dictated by the simple, architectonic approach of the craftsmen. Lively, individualized, full-length portraits are typical, as contrasted with the ornate three-quarter figures swathed in classical draperies characteristic of the more elegant English and Continental figureheads. American ship carvings were characteristically made of soft pine rather than of the oak, elm and other hard woods used abroad. The ease with which the pine could be cut abetted the American carvers' natural inclination to model their surfaces in broad planes, and to pay less attention to elaborate detail than to the large contours of the silhouette. The spare vigor and simple designs which distinguish our provincial painting are also characteristic of the ship carving. It is interesting to see this native style evolving through the years, from its beginnings in English-style work for the eighteenth-century Navy and merchant ships to the typically American carvings that decorated the whale ships and clippers of the nineteenth century. Because the carvers, unlike the painters, rarely went

LEVI L. CUSHING,
CARVER,
No 79, Broad Street, opposite Custom House Street,
BOSTON.
Orders for carved work of any description will be attended to with fidelity and despatch.
L. L. Cushing continues the above business in Poplar Street, as usual, where orders will meet with prompt attention. ☞N. B....Models of any kind executed at the shortest notice.

3.   Trade Card of Levi L. Cushing

abroad to study, and because their art sprang from and remained in the craft rather than the fine arts tradition, there was a minimum dilution of native style with imported academic fashion.

There has been a widespread tendency to value early American art in direct proportion to its antiquity—with a general assumption that eighteenth-century

American paintings and sculpture were superior in quality to those of the nineteenth. The basis for this is the traditional criticism of American art according to English standards, and hence the favoring of eighteenth-century work when these standards were most closely adhered to. Following the Declaration of Independence a distinct way of life and a parallel home-grown style in the arts began to thrive in America. This native art was democratically attuned to the tastes of the masses, whereas the elegant English-style art had made its appeal to a select few. The figureheads of this period are generally considered "crude" in comparison with the earlier and more finished sculptures of Rush and his school. They are indeed cruder, but in a positive sense. They are bolder and stronger, and are closer to the pioneering spirit of American life.

These native carvings were produced by craftsmen ignorant of Old-World custom and untrained according to academic standards. The period—the late eighteenth and the nineteenth century—was that in which America came into its own as a nation, when its national life, and so its art, expressed the realization of American independence won in the Revolution. The best of the ship figureheads are free, original, vigorous expressions of the very spirit of the flowering American democracy. As such they are highly significant in the history of American art.

4. Lady with a Rose

5. Figurehead   6. Victorian Lady

7.   Belle of Bath

(Reproduced in color inside back cover)

8. Lady with Scarf

9. Columbia   10. Lady with Umbrella

11. Columbia

12. Andrew Jackson   13. Figurehead of Ship *Creole*

14. **Binnacle Figure**   15. **Indian Chief**

16. Sailor   17. George R. Skolfield

18. General Peter B. Porter

19. Stern Decoration from Ship *Columbia*

20.   Eagle Figurehead

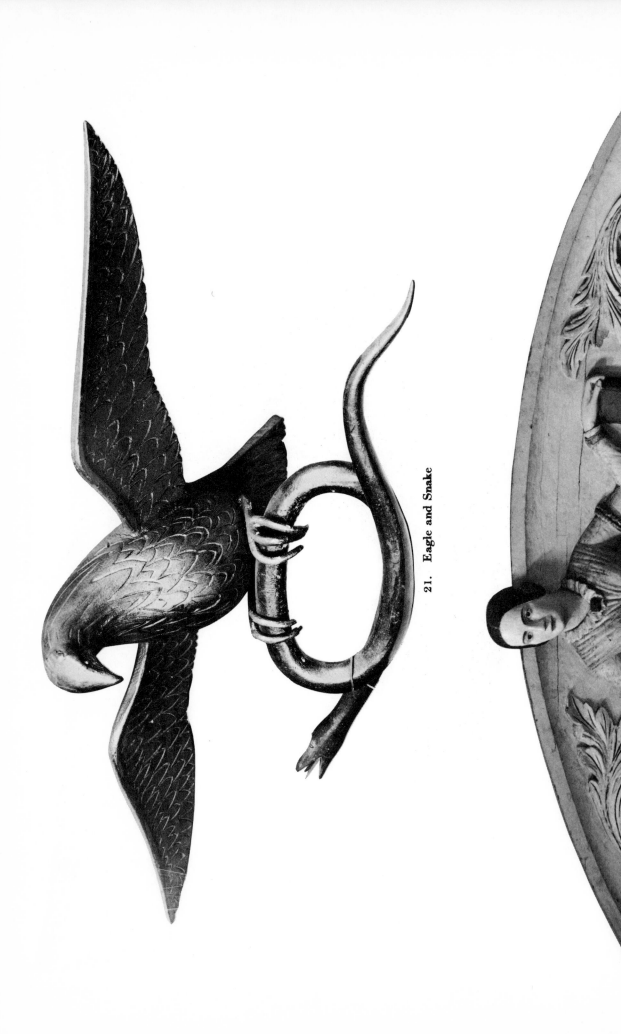

21. Eagle and Snake

22. Eunice Adams

23. Sternpiece

24. Stern Carving from Ship *American Indian*

WEATHERVANES

THE ORIGIN of the weathervane may be traced back to Athens, in the year 100 B.C., when Andronicus built his Tower of Winds and crowned it with a bronze Triton which pointed a wand in the direction of the wind. In England weathervanes were used from the time of William the Conqueror, and after the French Revolution they were common throughout Europe. It is interesting to find that in early times the Scandinavians used weathervanes on ships.

American vanes are recorded from the seventeenth century. About the first one known is the copper cockerel made in 1656 for the Dutch Reformed Church at Albany. One of the oldest American weathervanes to be seen is the wooden codfish studded with copper nails which was originally on Paul Revere's coppersmith shop in Canton, Massachusetts, and which is now on display at the Paul Revere House in Boston. The Indian and weathercock made by Shem Drowne for the Province House and the New Brick Church in Boston both date from the first quarter of the eighteenth century. A number of early Indian archers cut out of sheet iron have been preserved, most of which have been found in Pennsylvania (Figs. 28, 29, 31). Cockerels were popular as church vanes from earliest times, and a number of eighteenth-century examples have survived. By the mid-nineteenth century weathervane designs were legion. From the middle to the end of the century weathervanes were made in large numbers, still carved of wood or cut out of sheet metal in silhouette, as in earlier times, by artisans in rural districts, and cast in iron or molded of sheet copper by the large weathervane companies.

The first known professional weathervane maker was "Deacon" Shem Drowne, a coppersmith born in Boston in 1683, who was also a carver of pump heads, mantelpiece decorations, trade signs, and figureheads. In Hawthorne's story of *Drowne's Wooden Image* he describes the copper Indian which topped the old Province House, the former residence of the royal governors of the Colony (Fig. 30): "An Indian chief, gilded all over, stood during the better part of a century on the cupola of the Province House, bedazzling the eyes of those who looked upward, like an angel in the sun." Tradition records that crowds of children used to gather about the Province House at mid-day to watch for the fulfilment of the legend that the Indian would shoot his arrow at high noon. This superstition has long been forgotten, and now children and grownups as well come to the Massachusetts Historical Society to see the fierce Indian at close range.

The huge copper cockerel made for the New Brick Church on Hanover Street in Boston about 1722, now on the First Church in Cambridge, is an impressive Drowne weathervane. His most famous vane, however, is the hammered copper grasshopper with green glass eyes, which he made in his Ann Street shop in 1749 for the cupola of Faneuil Hall and which is still in place today. This vane, here illustrated (Fig. 25), and one which he made for Peter Faneuil's summer home, were copies of the grasshopper topping the Royal Exchange in London. They in turn were copied more than a hundred years later by L. W. Cushing & Sons, a

25. Grasshopper

weathervane company in Waltham, Massachusetts. This huge insect was one of the most interesting nineteenth-century models, and is now eagerly sought by collectors.

J. Rayner Whipple, in an article written for *Old-Time New England*, details the history of the amazingly durable Faneuil Hall grasshopper and quotes a paper found attached to it during one of the several times it underwent minor repairs. The early account records, not too accurately but most intimately, its origin and early history:

> Shem Drowne made it May 25, 1742. To my brethren and fellow Grasshopper: Fell in ye year 1753 Nov. 18, early in ye morning by a great earthquake by my Old Master above. . . . Again like to have met with my Utter Ruin by fire, but hopping Timely from my Public Scituation cam of with Broken bones and much Bruised. Cured and fixed. . . . (by) Old Master's son Thomas Drowne June 28, 1768, and though I will promise to Discharge my Office, yet I shall vary as ye wind.

One James Lombard, a nineteenth-century Maine weathervane carver, was typical of the later craftsmen who produced the useful sculpture we now treasure as folk art. Lombard was born in Baldwin, Maine, in 1865, attended school there and then removed to Bridgton. During his youth he is said to have made a large number of weathervanes. He was a farmer by profession, and an amateur furniture and weathervane maker. The fact that a number of the hen and rooster vanes in which he specialized have been found on barns as far away as Wells, Maine, suggests that he may have enjoyed a brief itinerant career in his youth, earning his way by carving weathervanes as he traveled the Maine highways. The weathered wood rooster which was painted white many years ago (Fig. 32) came from the barn of the Lombard homestead in Bridgton, while the hen which retains a more recent coat of white paint (Fig. 33) was found on a hen house in Wells. An original layer of yellow ochre is discernible on both pieces, and it seems likely that this color was the economical country cousin of the gold leaf used for contemporary metal vanes. Both hen and rooster were simply sawed and chiseled from thick slabs of pine, to which yellow painted wooden legs were attached. The silhouettes of these weathervanes and others Lombard executed are extremely stylized, and the cut-out areas which indicate the arrangement of tail feathers greatly enhance the interest of the design. The white hen with straight yellow legs and bold black eye, seen in profile against the sky, with blue showing through the large hole and small crescent slits, was a jaunty bit of decoration that enlivened the whole farm landscape. The effect achieved through a flair for functional design and a natural vitality of execution, as seen in these provincial weathervanes, would be hard to surpass in the most finished pieces of academic sculpture.

After 1850 the majority of weathervanes for churches, barns, houses, and public buildings were manufactured in factories rather than made by artisans. The large-scale production of metal weathervanes was quite a thriving industry during the second half of the century. In 1853 the J. W. Fiske Works began quantity manufacture in New York and several big companies followed suit, among them L. W. Cushing & Sons of Waltham, Massachusetts; W. A. Snow Co., Inc., John A. Whim and J. Harris & Son of Boston; and J. L. Mott of New York. Their old catalogues give a good idea of their wares. A page from an early Snow Co. catalogue is here reproduced (Fig. 26). Besides plain bannerets, feathers, arrows, and copper balls, thousands of horses, eagles, cocks, Columbias, and countless other subjects were turned out, mostly of sheet copper and cast iron. The copper weathervanes, when new, must have added a glittering accent to the serene countryside. It is significant that in many primitive landscape paintings weathervanes are prominently depicted in oversized proportions. Weather was of course the basic factor in rural life, and so the weathervane was an accessory of major importance.

During the seventeenth and eighteenth centuries the subjects of weathervanes were limited to a few designs—simple arrows, fish, cocks, Indians, serpents, and grasshoppers. By the nineteenth century there were scores of subjects, which reflect all the special and localized interests of the American people, and all the themes that attracted them as a nation.

The farmers' attention focused on the livestock of the farm, and for barn and hen-house weathervanes they chose mostly horses, cows, sheep, pigs, and poultry. In the seacoast villages one finds old weathervanes representing sailors, ships,

whales, seagulls, and fish of various kinds. On churches everywhere the gilded
weathercock turned in silhouette as sign of the cock that crowed the night Peter

GAME COCK WITH ARROW.

WYANDOTTE. (New Pattern.)

ROOSTERS.

ROOSTERS.

GAME COCK.

VESSELS.

FISH.

PEN.

26.   Illustrations from Old Weathervane Catalogue

denied the Lord, and in New England the fish frequently replaced the cock as a
churchtop symbol. Gabriel blowing his trumpet and a stylized lyre were equally
popular as ecclesiastical vanes. Some weathervanes were flown as special markers

for public buildings, a fireman or engine for the local firehouse for example; and some were actual trade signs in the form of weathervanes. Among the interesting trade-sign vanes that have been found are a plow for a large farm, a gloved hand pointing to the wind over a glove factory, a mortar and pestle for an apothecary, and the unique pig on a butcher's knife made for Captain David West's slaughterhouse in Fairhaven, Massachusetts (Fig. 45). Large ram weathervanes still mark many old woolen mills.

In New England, which prided itself on its shipbuilding, ship weathervanes were frequently flown. In eastern Pennsylvania, where hex signs were painted on barns to ward off ill-intentioned witches, we find that in pioneer times many barns displayed sheet-iron Indian weathervanes, which are said to have been a practical means of keeping marauding Indians away by indicating amity between the white man and the Indian. The Indian made an ideal weathervane subject from the point of view of design too, as the arrow accurately pointed in the direction of the wind. Whirligigs, like the Quakertown example illustrated in Fig. 47, are another kind of weathervane typical of Pennsylvania.

Weathervane subjects popular everywhere were a horse and sulky designed after a Currier and Ives print, jockeys on horseback, dogs, wild animals like deer, squirrels and pheasants, and locomotives and steamboats. Among the most widely used weathervanes, and most interesting as representative of a native art, were those that took the forms of the well-loved American emblems—Columbia, Liberty, the American eagle, and Uncle Sam. In England weathervanes were commonly made in aristocratic heraldic designs. The patriotic American vanes which topped simple homes and fine public buildings and rural schoolhouses constituted what Rita Wellman, writing of weathervane designs for *House Beautiful*, designates as "a new and ingratiating heraldry, a heraldry of democracy."

There are also subjects found in a scattered few or single examples only—a centaur, sea horse, Mercury, Diana, dragon, Revolutionary officer, man bowling, country preacher on horseback, hunting dogs chasing a fox, an eagle with a fish in its talons, an Indian shooting a deer which is a unique weathervane landscape (Fig. 44). A swan, ostrich, crane, peacock, pigeon, donkey, bullfrog, and fox are among the rare animal subjects.

Weathervane techniques are as varied as the subjects. The wooden vanes were carved with chisels or cut out of flat planks with small saws. They were almost invariably painted for protection from the weather. Some were painted in a solid color, most often Indian red, or yellow ochre to simulate gilded metal, or white. Often the vanes were polychromed, which added to the interest of the design. The female angel wearing high black boots (Fig. 39) is painted in staccato black and white, with a brassy yellow trumpet. The wooden Indian who shoots off his own arm as an arrow (Fig. 27) is painted dark red with red, yellow and white striping down the sides and around the neck and arms to indicate the borders of his dress. His headdress is yellow, the round eye is circled in black and white and the wire bow is painted black.

The metal vanes were also sometimes painted, often gilded. Yellow ochre doubled for gold leaf over copper, and some dark color was commonly used to preserve the surface of flat iron silhouettes. Sometimes too the sheet-iron vanes were polychromed like the Indian archer and the fireman reproduced (Figs. 31, 49). The majority of the metal vanes were, however, left unpainted. The copper ones shone brightly in the sun, even when not covered with gold leaf, and when they became dull and greened over with verdigris they could be gilded at any time.

The metal vanes were cut and cast and modeled in a variety of ways. The simplest technique was to cut a silhouette from a flat sheet of iron, zinc or tin. In Pennsylvania an anonymous weathervane maker habitually separated two identical tin profiles with an inch-wide ribbon of tin, soldered the edges, and so achieved a flat but interestingly three-dimensional shape. During the late nineteenth century when cast-iron units for fences, gates and trellises were being manufactured in large quantity, iron was commonly cast in sand molds for weathervanes. For the animal vanes sheet-iron tails were frequently applied to the heavy, rounded bodies. The fine rooster and horse (Figs. 36, 41), which appear to have been designed by one artisan, were made in this way. The majority of the nineteenth-century vanes were of sheet copper, fashioned on an iron pattern cast from a carved wood model or hammered up and chiseled on a plain block of wood or lead. The two sides, modeled in the round or half-round, were then joined with solder. Sometimes details such as a fish's fins or a horse's or rooster's tail were cut out of sheet copper, chiseled into the proper surface design and applied in silhouette to the rounded body. In some copper weathervanes parts were made of cast iron or zinc to add weight. An example of this mixed technique is the Goddess of Liberty reproduced in Fig. 46 in which a cast zinc torso is combined with a molded copper skirt and a cut-out brass flag. The grasshopper made by the Cushing company combines cast zinc legs and antennae and leg filaments of brass tubing with a sheet copper body.

An unusual relic of the old weathervane industry is a wooden model (Fig. 40) made for the casting of an iron pattern. The pattern or template was then used for fashioning sheets of copper into the rounded form of this spirited horse with the fox-like tail.

The techniques of the weathervane makers had a great deal to do with the character of the finished vanes. Except for the cast-iron pieces the work was finished entirely by hand, and striking individual differences are seen even in pieces modeled on the same template. The finishing of the sheet-copper vanes with chiseled decoration left the sculptor free to follow his inclinations in the realm of design. The copper rooster (Fig. 34), where variations in the feathers are indicated by a kind of sculptural shorthand, is an outstanding example of conventionalized weathervane design.

The functional use of the weathervane, too, dictated an emphasis on pattern rather than on illusionistic realism; for the piece was intended to be seen at a distance, clearly silhouetted against the sky to indicate wind direction at a glance. It is only necessary to compare a group of animal weathervanes with contemporary animal paintings and drawings to see how dramatically the weathervane makers enhanced the natural design characteristic of the profiled objects. It seems obvious that the great popularity of cock and horse weathervanes, which far outnumber any other subjects, was conditioned by the prevalence of these domesticated animals, but may also have had something to do with the inherent decorative interest of the silhouettes of a running horse and strutting cock.

Alfred Barr's book on Picasso quotes the great painter's statement: "Cocks have always been seen, but never as well as in American weather vanes.'' It is significant that Picasso, who had never been in America at the time he made this remark, should have been so much aware of the quality of our simple, native weathervane designs. The average person is inclined to be most immediately attracted to the naïve, story-telling vanes, like the mare with tiny foal, the Indian shooting a deer, or the man driving a pig (Figs. 42, 44, 45). But it is rather those simpler pieces that one feels could stand up as pure design in comparison with any sculpture, native or foreign, primitive or academic, that will retain the most lasting value as American folk art.

The painted sheet-iron Indian archer (Fig. 31) looks as if he must have been designed by someone who had never seen any conventional art. The minute hands and feet and the oversized eye with pierced eyebrow set high up in the forehead give the figure a strangely primitive look. The silhouette is intricate and lively, with the large zig-zag motif of the headdress and feathered skirt repeated as sharp minor rhythms in the edges of trousers, hair, and quiver of arrows, in the amazing saw-toothed arm and tiny sharp fingers. The pierced areas which mark brow, ear and neck are as abstract in shape as the units of the open-work design which serves as a base for the figure.

The sheet-iron Diana (Fig. 38) presents another fascinating profile, complex and beautifully balanced. The line flows around the head, wings, and body with interestingly varied rhythm. The strong vertical lines of the supporting rod and the exactly horizontal arrow establish a sense of stability, and emphasize by contrast the rounded contours of the figure. This weathervane was certainly not designed with these aesthetic principles in mind, but the maker instinctively wrought his figure with a dynamic balance of lines and masses, which resolve themselves into a rich formal pattern for our design-conscious modern eye.

The formal iron horse, of which Fig. 41 is one of a number of castings, is generally considered one of the finest examples of American folk sculpture and has been compared with ancient Chinese and Greek statuettes. The strong sculptural feeling and the suggestion of the muscular tension of a spirited animal combine to give this piece a restrained power that is immediately communicated to the spectator.

The gilded-copper Goddess of Liberty (Fig. 46) is another unquestionable masterpiece. It is dramatically designed, with the flying flag balancing the out-stretched left arm, and the flagpole establishing a strong vertical axis for the figure. Fortunately a number of versions of this outstanding weathervane design have been preserved.

The iron pheasant (Fig. 43) is the simplest imaginable weathervane, and yet it strikes one as among the finest examples of American design. If one of our modern sculptors had conceived this piece one would talk of sophisticated simplification; actually its purity of line was the result of the unselfconscious instinct for design that guided the shears of some simple Pennsylvania ironsmith.

27. Indian Archer

28. Indian Archer

29.   Indian Archer

30.   Indian Archer

31.   Indian Archer

32. Rooster

33. Hen

35. Rooster

34. Crowing Cock

36. Rooster

37. Swordfish

38. Diana

39. Angel

40. Model for Horse

41. Formal Horse

42.   Mare and Foal

43.   Pheasant

44.   Indian Shooting Deer

45.   Man Driving Pig

46.   Goddess of Liberty

47. Whirligig

48. Liberty

49. Fireman

CIGAR-STORE FIGURES
AND OTHER TRADE SIGNS

THE OLD carved trade signs—a boot to mark a cobbler, or an Indian for a cigar-store—are the homely antecedents of the advertising art of our day. Figures carved as appropriate eye-catchers for all kinds of shops, taverns, and public buildings record in concrete form the typical occupations and fashions of a past era. Collections of early metal fire-marks formerly attached to insured houses re-create the history of the primitive fire brigades. Swift-flying eagles and leaping Indian braves, used as trademark decorations on the first fast trains, dramatize the pioneer beginnings of modern cross-country travel. The trade signs reproduced in the following plates were all objects of everyday use in their time. They merit attention today as outstanding examples of folk sculpture, and as vital documents of many aspects of the American past in which they played a functional part.

The cigar-store figures are the most varied and picturesque of American trade signs. The cigar-store Indian, symbol of our first pioneer, has had an especially noteworthy career, from his early days as the most popular of the shop signs to his twentieth-century eminence as a collectors' item.

The genealogy of the cigar-store Indian goes back to seventeenth-century England. Sir Walter Raleigh is said to have brought tobacco home from his trip to America, told his countrymen of the Peace Pipe and the joys of smoking, and so introduced the "Indian weed" to England. The earliest tobacco-shop Indian was a strange hybrid. He was portrayed as a negro with a feathered headdress wearing a kilt of tobacco leaves, and was known as a "Virginian." This odd character is accounted for by the fact that the English had apparently confused the American Indian who first smoked tobacco, the Virginian from whom the tobacco was imported, and the plantation darky who raised the crop. In America the Indian was not established as a cigar-store sign until the middle of the nineteenth century. A few were undoubtedly carved before this time, and the archaic squaw shown in Fig. 63 is probably one of the earliest specimens. The heyday of the Indian was from the fifties through the eighties. In his native land he was accurately carved and painted—a fierce chief brandishing a tomahawk, a squaw with fine, feathered headdress and beads, sometimes carrying a papoose, an occasional fur trapper with his equipment.

The most authentic account of cigar-store signs is to be found in an article which Frank Weitenkampf wrote for the *New York Times* in 1890. This article is largely based on the reminiscences of Samuel Robb of New York, a carver active in the trade for a quarter of a century. It seems that the earliest wooden Indians were designed and carved by the makers of figureheads who, with the decay of American shipping, had lost their occupation and turned to the making of cigar-store figures. We may observe that these early figures were more originally designed and less statically posed than the later ones. They were not modeled after book illustrations or prints, but were individual in conception and displayed the same vitality of workmanship and bold distribution of color that distinguish the figureheads.

The Indian with the tomahawk (Fig. 60) is one of the few recorded as made by a known figurehead carver. A letter from a former owner of this figure, in whose family it had been since 1857, states that the Indian was long ago identified by a Mr. Cromwell, through a stamped trademark, as the work of his father, John L. Cromwell of Williamsburg, New York. The Pinckney book on figureheads lists John L. Cromwell as a ship carver, with shop address in 1840 at 419 Water Street, New York City. According to Cromwell's son his father used to carve figureheads for sailing vessels, and when steamboats began to take their place he bought up the big spars and out of them carved Indians for cigar stores. It is interesting to see that he represented this Indian's headdress and cloak as blown by the wind in characteristic figurehead style.

The Indian trapper in the Williamsburg collection (Fig. 59) is another prime example of the relatively early carvings. There is the same suggestion of dynamic action in the pose that one senses in the figureheads; the trapper, though momentarily at ease, seems poised to spring. The designer transformed a solid block of wood into an animate figure with flowing contours, and he tooled the surface with bold strokes and colored it simply in wide areas of green, red, yellow ochre, and brown. The boldness of design, breadth of handling and richness of color combine to make this figure a dashing piece of native sculpture.

The price range around 1890 is given as from sixteen dollars for a small counter Indian to a hundred and twenty-five for a large figure. These figures were generally carved in the cities of the eastern seaboard and the largest number came from the workshops of Samuel Robb and Thomas White in New York. The painted metal Indians began to succeed the wooden ones in the late eighties. They were expensive, but extremely weather-resistant and so heavy that they were difficult to steal. They were more realistic in pose and detail than the wooden Indians and, being cast, characteristically lacked the bold, individual style that made the earlier carved ones so arresting. Toward the end of the century a number of pewter and zinc Indians were manufactured by Demuth & Co., an old New York tobacconist firm who advertised their metal figures as the first in that line (Fig. 50). Two of the pewter examples are preserved in the Everhart Museum in Scranton, one in the collection of Mrs. Walter White in Gates Mills, Ohio. Indians are also recorded as made of iron, lead, bronze, and even *papier mâché*. Such Indians, like the wooden profiles carved in low relief, of which there is an excellent example in the Rudolph Haffenreffer collection in Bristol, Rhode Island, are relatively rare specimens, but they are not as attractive from the point of view of folk sculpture as are the ordinary wooden varieties.

The method of the carvers is described by Weitenkampf as follows:

50.   Early Advertisement of William Demuth & Co.

The wood used is generally white pine, which is bought in logs of various lengths at the spar yards. The artist begins by making the roughest kind of an outline—a mere suggestion of what the proportions of the figure are to be. In this he is guided by paper patterns. The log is blocked out with the axe into appropriate spaces for the head, the body down to the waist, the portion from there to the knee, the rest of the legs (which are at once divided), and the feet. The feeling for form in the chopped block is so very elementary as to have complete suggestiveness only for the practiced artist. A hole is now bored in each end of the prepared log about 5 inches deep. Into each hole an iron bolt is placed, the projecting parts of which rest on supports so that the body hangs free. The carver now goes from the general to the particular. The surface of the wood soon becomes chipped up by the chisel and the log generally takes on more definite form. Then when the figure is completely evolved the finishing touches are put in with finer tools. Detached hands and arms are made separately and joined to the body with screws. Then the various portions are appropriately painted, the whole is set on a stand running on wheels, and it is ready for delivery.

Another old account of cigar-store Indians is given by Kate Sanborn in her amusing booklet entitled *Hunting Indians in a Taxi-cab,* which was published in 1911. The author quotes a Mr. Caspari of Calvert Street, the oldest tobacconist in Baltimore, who recalled many interesting facts and figures. He stated that a carved Indian was considered a necessary adjunct to the early tobacco business, and not till much later were the large assortment of other figure subjects popular. When he started in business his stock cost only thirty dollars, but he had an Indian out front that cost forty. He estimated that the pine figures had been finished by the carver in about a week. They were painted flashily with high-grade paint and trimmings of gold or silver, and were repainted every year or two. After the earliest days of small-scale production by native ship carvers many Swiss and German woodcarvers who had migrated to America turned to the carving of Indians. Toward the end of the century some first-rate American sculptors worked at this trade. Julius Theodore Melchers of Detroit was one, and he charged up to seven hundred dollars for his figures at a time when about a hundred-and-twenty-five was a high price. A fine Indian in Dr. A. W. Pendergast's collection in Terre Haute, Indiana, is accompanied by the original bill of sale for $467.50, dated 1857, indicating that it must have been made by an important carver.

An authoritative history of cigar-store Indians written by J. L. Morrison in 1928, when they were just beginning to be of real interest to collectors, adds to the earlier accounts a number of interesting facts that we should note. In detailing the history of the cigar-store Indian the writer illustrates the earliest American tobacco-shop figure, a delicate Colonial gentleman tendering a snuff box, which was made for Christopher Demuth's tobacco shop in Lancaster, Pennsylvania, in 1770, and which stands there to this day. He states that tradition records a few isolated eighteenth-century tobacco figures, but not till the 1840's is there actual evidence of an Indian used in America. Discussing the makers' techniques, he mentions that some figures were constructed entirely of small blocks glued together. He tells about the smallest Indians, made not only for counters but for window display, about thirty inches high, which were the specialty of a Brooklyn dealer who sold them in large quantities. Italians in New York also made and peddled small painted plaster Indians about two feet high for window use. It seems that a number of tobacconists, like Demuth & Co., carried on a flourishing business in wooden Indians as a sideline, and some of them did a large trade-in business exchanging newer for old models. Some itinerant painters, hard as it now is to believe, made a full-time profession of repainting these cigar-store figures. A few Indians were imported from France and Italy for America's sidewalks, and a number of native Indians, Mr. Morrison relates, were as widely traveled. He writes of an Indian figurehead which was removed from its ship to become a landlubber cigar-store figure, and of one Chief Semloh who, a New Yorker in origin, became a Californian. He was one of the Forty-niners, arriving in Maryville, California, in 1850 via Cape Horn, and in 1916 was taken to a tobacco shop in San Francisco. Where this wooden pioneer resides today is not known, but it would not be surprising to find him well cared for in a collection in Indiana or Rhode Island or back home in New York.

In the first decade of our century, when only a handful of people like Kate Sanborn and Frank Weitenkampf were actively interested in the history of wooden Indians, they were no longer so popular as signs; and local ordinances in many cities had outlawed them from the pavements where they were considered objectionable obstructions to the crowded sidewalks, especially when pedestrians bumping into them at night found they could sue the city for damages. They became the vanishing Americans, exterminated by the thousands by their owners as outmoded junk. It has been estimated that at one time there were about seventy-five thousand, and that after the cigar-store Indian massacre no more than three thousand survived. Gradually the scarce old Indians came to be valued as collectors' pieces, and now most of the surviving braves and squaws have been retired to reservations in private collections and museums. Since the earliest Indian hunts through city streets, when a good specimen could be bought for under fifty dollars, the status of the cigar-store Indian has radically changed. Numerous important collectors, museums and historical societies have joined the chase, and the current wampum for a good redskin is upwards of five hundred dollars.

There are quite a few picturesque collections of wooden Indians. At one time about a hundred examples were scattered throughout the wooded forest on an island estate along the Maine coast. Mr. Haffenreffer now houses more than twice that number in his King Philip's Museum at Bristol, Rhode Island. Dr. Pendergast of Terre Haute, Indiana, who owned two hundred and forty-three specimens a few years ago, recently disposed of almost two hundred, thirty-five of which were sold back into the trade to serve again as cigar-store signs. Besides collecting, he ran an "Indian Hospital" in which he performed major and minor operations to restore injured wooden Indians for museums and collectors. Dr. Pendergast has made a thorough study of the characteristics of these old Indians, and can tell at a glance whether a hole in the top of a squaw's head was intended to hold a missing cluster of feathers, or was made to contain oil which helped preserve the wood from decay. The flat top of a small counter Indian's feather headdress might look odd and in need of restoration to an amateur collector, but Dr. Pendergast would recognize this as a platform designed to display a box of cigars. He knows from his travels the typical Indian features so that he could accurately repair a damaged face, but he pointed out in a letter to this author that only a few of the men who carved the wooden Indians ever saw a live specimen. Very few of the figures, he says, even remotely resemble Indians; and the majority of squaws, excepting for their color and dress, look like any plain, buxom American girl.

Interest in wooden Indians remains active, which is reflected in the large amount of press publicity accorded them, and there exists at this time a unique club titled "The Society for the Preservation of the Cigar-Store Indian." It was founded by Capt. Miller Freeman, a Bellevue, Washington, newspaper editor who is its president. The membership requirement is possession of one or more wooden Indians or an altruistic interest in preserving the race. The chief aim of the society is to save the remaining Indians by helping to get them into the proper collections. The author's membership card is here reproduced (Fig. 51), and a portion of the letter which accompanied it is quoted below:

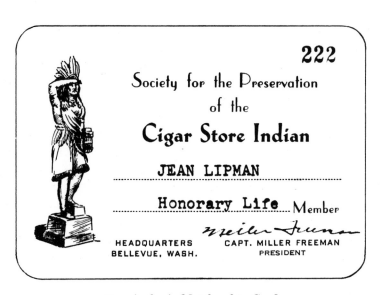

222

Society for the Preservation

of the

Cigar Store Indian

JEAN LIPMAN

Honorary Life Member

CAPT. MILLER FREEMAN
PRESIDENT

HEADQUARTERS
BELLEVUE, WASH.

51. Author's Membership Card

You will find this card of special value to you—in fact, you can throw away all your other identification cards. Evidence of affiliation with THIS Society will get you in anywhere; getting out is your own problem.

Let me hasten to add that there are no initiation fees, no dues, or obligations of any kind in connection with membership in our organization. You are expected, however, to scout diligently for genuine hand-carved wooden Indians and report on any you find to the President, at headquarters, Bellevue, Washington.

An invitation to a club dinner in 1946 stated: "No English spoken. All communications in Chinook, by smoke signals or sign language. Also tomahawk-throwing and scalp-lifting contests." It seems clear that this society is well worth joining!

The parade of carved figures which followed the early vogue for Indians as cigar-store signs presents a vivid contemporary picture of all the personalities close to the hearts of the people in the latter part of the nineteenth century. A Vermont collector of cigar-store figures believes there is scarcely a typical character that was not immortalized in wood, holding cigars, snuff, or tobacco leaves to advertise a tobacco shop. We can list only some of the commonest types, and have reproduced a few representative examples. There were the picturesque foreigners: Turk, Egyptian, Scotchman, Amazon. There were representatives of America's everyday folk: baseball player, preacher, trapper, Civil War soldier, sailor, jockey, race-track tout, dandy, lady of fashion, policeman, bandmaster, and the roustabout darky of steamboat days, used principally along the Mississippi and Ohio rivers. An elderly owner of a cigar store on Third Avenue in New York had himself carved in the uniform of the shooting company to which he belonged, so we may include at least one portrait of a cigar-store keeper among the cigar-store figures.

There were popular characters of folklore and history: Punch, Columbine, Puck, Byron, Lord Dundreary, Sir Walter Raleigh, Champagne Charlie, Andrew Jackson, Daniel Webster, the Zouave and the Forty-niner. Then there were the personsified symbols of the U.S.A.: Uncle Sam, Columbia, Liberty, Yankee Doodle. There were portraits of prominent personages of the day: Edwin Forrest the actor, John L. Sullivan, Dolly Varden, Jenny Lind, Admiral Dewey, and Henry Ward Beecher in his pulpit.

There is preserved a lively portrait of the negro preacher, the Reverend Campbell (Fig. 75), which was ordered by Alan Pinkerton, the famous detective, to honor the memory of this "paid servant" who had lived on his estate. According to Mr. Robert Kuhn, who now owns this remarkable carving, Pinkerton—Lincoln's personal bodyguard during the Civil War—was, like Henry Ward Beecher, very much opposed to slavery. He was filling out papers to free his slaves as fast as he could, and asked the Rev. Campbell to preach to all his colored people, while they waited for their "freedom papers." The slaves, it seems, didn't respect Campbell because, except for his wide collar, he dressed just as they did. Pinkerton solved this problem on a trip to Chicago when he saw some hotel doormen impressively dressed in long, red plush coats, bought one for Campbell, and told him that was what all ministers wore. From that time on he had great prestige on the estate, and always wore the fine red coat in which he appears today, with his carpet bag and umbrella. This likeness stood in the Pinkerton manor house in Onarga, Illinois, until it was sold and the figure became the property of a cigar-store owner. Since that time it has been shipped about to advertise all sorts of conventions, becoming a unique example of an itinerant trade sign.

One of the most unusual folk carvings is the portrait of Mark Twain's Colonel Sellers, the super promoter of *The Gilded Age* (Fig. 68). He is shown in one of his typical peaks of enthusiasm as he extolls some sure-thing notion with "oceans of money in it." It is probably "Beriah Sellers' Infallible Imperial Oriental Optic Liniment and Salvation for Sore Eyes—the Medical Wonder of the Age," for this dramatic figure was an apothecary shop sign. It came from Sellersville, Pennsylvania, a town which would quite naturally have taken a special interest in Colonel Sellers.

Wooden figures were used in America as signs for all sorts of shops. Among the commonest, in the late eighteenth and early nineteenth centuries, were the little carved mariners who advertised the seaport ship chandlers and instrument makers. Hawthorne mentions in *Drowne's Wooden Image* that Shem Drowne, the famous eighteenth-century sculptor whom we discussed in connection with his weathervanes, made a carved figure of his friend Captain Hunnewell holding a quadrant and a telescope, which attracted attention to the shop of a nautical instrument maker in Boston. A similar sign used to hang in front of the Crown Coffee House in Boston in 1770 to advertise William Williams, maker of mathematical instruments. A fine example of this type of sign, probably the work of a local ship carver, is the navigator who hung over the street door of James Fales' nautical instrument shop in New Bedford (Fig. 81).

The sculptor who executed this figure, and another one of a mariner holding a telescope which is in the author's collection, was undoubtedly self-taught. He had developed his own unconventional formula for proportioning and modeling figures, carving hair and painting faces. He was endowed with a vigorous sense of plastic design, a bold, forthright technique, and a flair for robust color combinations. The quality of design in the navigator is apparent in the plate. The low-relief carving for the details of clothing and hair may not be clearly apparent in reproduction. It deserves comment because of the manner in which the sculptor has added interest to his forms with carved detail which, however, he has kept strictly subordinated to the large planes and contours of his figure.

These carvings are closely related to primitive English signs such as the wooden midshipman which Dickens describes in *Dombey and Son,* published in 1847–48. This figure, adorning old Sol Gill's shop, "thrust itself out above the pavement, right leg foremost" and "bore at its right eye the most offensively disproportionate piece of machinery." He was, Dickens tells us, one of many "little timber midshipmen in obsolete naval uniform, eternally employed outside the shop-doors of nautical instrument-makers in taking observations of the hackney-coaches."

It is because a large part of the early population of our country was presumably illiterate that we have such a fascinating collection of carved trade signs today. There were primitive figures advertising early bars and taverns (Figs. 66, 79) and inn signs carved in relief on wood and stone. A representation of an arm holding a bell, carved in the round, was the homely sign for the "Bell in Hand" temperance tavern run by James Wilson, an old town crier in Boston. The tavern, popular in the early nineteenth century, was in the basement of the Exchange Coffee House fronting on what is now Congress Square. Toward the end of the nineteenth century an occasional city restaurant keeper ordered a wooden figure of one of the popular cigar-store types, such as a baseball player, had the base lettered with the name of his restaurant and placed it on the sidewalk to attract the attention of passers-by. Weathervane trade signs were mentioned in the preceding chapter. Cobblers, watchmakers, apothecary shops, milliners, blacksmiths, saddlers, glove-makers, hardware dealers, and countless other tradesmen had appropriate carved figures or plaques standing or hanging in front of their shops (Figs. 68, 73, 82). A Pennsylvania bootmaker advertised ladies' riding boots by means of the carving reproduced in Fig. 71. This large, meek hobbyhorse with its sidesaddle rider ranks with the outstanding examples of folk sculpture in any field. A tinsmith from Torrington, Connecticut, had as his sign a handsome peacock made in sections of hammered sheet zinc and copper soldered together. In New York a photographer's shop displayed a carved female figure holding a lens, and a firm dealing in rags had the figure of a ragman, nine feet high, placed on top of its building in Franklin Street. Other prominent pieces of advertising sculpture that became landmarks in our grand-parents' time were the enormous wooden cow that was milked daily on Coney Island, and the great elephant and gilded calf that ornamented the exteriors of two Tenth Avenue saloons in New York.

Public buildings too had carved figures which served as signs. The manacled felon from the Kent County Jail in East Greenwich, Rhode Island (Fig. 76), is an early example, which must have served as a warning as well as an identification for the townspeople. Courthouses occasionally displayed a large figure of Justice outside or inside the building. Fire departments were sometimes distinguished by appropriate figures, such as the huge portrait in wood of Harry Howard, Chief of the New York Volunteers (Fig. 74), or the fireman weathervane reproduced as Fig. 49. A carved representation of Saint Florian, who probably served as Patron Saint for some firehouse, is now in the Haffenreffer collection. This piece, related to cigar-store figures in type, is a delightful nineteenth-century American adaptation of a medieval German sculpture. The little black-enamelled figure holds a tilted water bucket and stands with one foot on the peaked rooftop of a burning house in much the same pose as cigar-store Indians stand with a foot on a pile of cigar boxes.

52. First Insignia of the Insurance
Company of North America

The fire-mark represents a unique category of folk art, attractive to collectors because of the wide variety of interesting designs in which the small metal plates were cast. They represent the earliest insurance company signs, designed to be prominently placed on buildings in order to distinguish the insured structures and to identify the insuring companies. Fire-marks were first used in England in the late seventeenth century, when each insurance company had its own fire brigade. The mark served to save firemen needless exercise, for the brigades only rushed to fight fires in buildings which their company insured and which were so identified by the company's mark.

In America the first fire insurance company was formed in 1752, under the inspiration of Benjamin Franklin who had organized the first fire brigade in 1735. This company, which is still in existence, was named the Philadelphia Contributionship for the Insurance of Houses from Loss by Fire. Its mark, designed by John Stow of Philadelphia, consisted of four crossed lead hands mounted on a wooden shield (Fig. 85). Because of its insignia it became popularly known as the "Hand-in-Hand." In 1792 the Insurance Company of North America was formed as the first fire and marine insurance company and adopted a lead star mounted on a wooden shield, here reproduced, for its mark (Fig. 52). As other companies sprang up new marks appeared, and the old companies issued newly designed plates until there were dozens of varieties.

Unlike the English, the American companies did not maintain their own brigades but relied on the volunteer fire companies already in existence. As insurance firms often favored certain fire brigades to whose support they contributed, the mark was helpful in securing full cooperation from these firemen. The mark also indicated that any brigade extinguishing a fire would be rewarded by the insuring company, and so competition waxed fierce when an insured house caught fire. The first brigade on the scene had traditional right of way and was entitled to the full reward unless it called for aid, which it was naturally reluctant to do, so that many a fire got the better of a lone unit when two or three could have subdued it. If the race to the scene of the fire resulted in a tie between several brigades, priority rights were settled with fists while the fire blazed away in the background. Should a race end in front of a burning house with no fire-mark, and so no guaranteed reward, the firemen would promptly depart and report a false alarm—a cold-blooded custom that must have accumulated business for the insurance companies. Toward the third quarter of the century paid fire departments began to succeed the volunteers, and from that time the fire-marks lost their function. They were then generally discontinued, though some companies still placed their trademark plates on insured houses purely for advertising purposes.

The Insurance Company of North America has assembled a hundred and seventeen old American fire-marks from eighteen states, dating from 1752. They make up the most complete collection in existence. The fire-marks here reproduced (Figs. 83–88) are all in this collection, which is open to public view in the company's main office in Philadelphia. The first insignia of the Insurance Company of North America was a lead star nailed to a wooden shield, and this fire-mark exists in a solitary example. It was found in 1929 after a systematic search instigated by the discovery of a stain on a house in Philadelphia which was exactly the same shape as the shield of the star mark, no specimen of which had been seen since 1879. Tracing back from the present owner of the building to his grandfather, the shield was finally discovered—with the faint outline of a star, but no star. The old man recalled nothing more than that the star had been sold to a second-hand dealer from Baltimore. The end of this tale of collector's luck (which highlights the point that "luck" is generally attributable to the perseverance of the collector) is that every junk shop in Baltimore was ransacked and the old star was eventually found. It exactly fitted the wooden shield, and today is the rarest of all fire-marks. Other stars have been offered for sale but scientific examination has proven them to be forgeries.

It is interesting to compare the English and American fire-marks. The plainness of the American designs and workmanship as contrasted with the elegance of the English is striking, and was remarked by Harold Gillingham in his article in *Antiques* on "The Fascinating Fire Mark." The American examples are all of sturdy design, quite crude, but vigorous and well-balanced in effect. The English plates are relatively delicate, with pierced open-work lightening the solid metal. Interest focuses on fine internal detail while in the American examples the emphasis is on the basic design. It is significant to find that even in such apparently

53. Aberdeen and Rockfish Engine Number 35

homogeneous objects as fire-marks a fundamental difference between English and American style is apparent.

The exterior trademark decorations for short-line railroads are one branch of folk sculpture that has only recently come to notice. Lucius Beebe, writing of "railroad art" in his *Mixed Train Daily,* draws attention to this phase of American design, which deserves the consideration of those who appreciate the qualities of nineteenth-century folk art. The bronze eagles for smokebox doors and iron cut-out Indian warriors and braves for headlight ornaments are railroad trademarks in the tradition of the early, individualistic trade signs (Fig. 53). The eagle here reproduced could have been derived from some earlier ship ornament—perhaps from a carved pilot-house eagle which topped a steamboat—while the silhouetted Indian is clearly a lineal descendant of a primitive Indian archer weathervane (see Fig. 29). It is interesting to see that the most dynamic designs for American eagles and Indians were adopted as decorative symbols for the new era of speed.

54.　Cigar-Store Indian

55 & 56.   Cigar-Store Indian

57. Cigar-Store Indian

58. "Seneca John"

59. Trapper Indian

60. Cigar-Store Indian   61. Cigar-Store Indian

62. Indian Maid   63. Squaw

64. Lady of Fashion

65. Cigar-Store Indian

66. Man with Grapes

67. Baseball Player

68. "Col. Sellers"

69. Darky   70. Dancing Darky

71. Bootmaker's Sign

72. Captain Jinks of the Horse Marines   73. Milliner's Sign

74. Harry Howard, Chief of the
New York Volunteer Fire Department

75.   Rev. Campbell   76.   Jail Sign

77. Sailor   78. Race Track Tout

79. Tavern Sign

80. Policeman

81. Navigator

82. Blacksmith's Shop Sign

83. Fire-Mark

84. Fire-Mark

86. Fire-Mark

85. Fire-Mark

88. Fire-Mark

87. Fire-Mark

CIRCUS AND CARROUSEL CARVINGS

THE PRIMITIVE CIRCUS which was the ancestor of the elaborate modern performance was a simple itinerant show. The great circus on tour had its humble origin in the eighteenth-century showman who, with a couple of trained or strange animals, entertained roadside tap-room audiences. The next stage in the history of the circus was the caravan with tent, menagerie and acrobats traveling in wagons for stop-over performances. The railroad and showboat circuses came next, touring cross-country in their own cars and down river in their showboats. This history of the evolution of the modern circus is discussed in detail in a chapter of Richardson Wright's *Hawkers and Walkers in Early America*. The recently opened Museum of the American Circus on the Ringling estate at Sarasota, Florida, provides an opportunity to see at first hand some of the accessories of the old circuses.

Most of the carvings which this chapter illustrates came into being in connection with early circus publicity. Posters, for one thing, were printed in quantity on large sheets from carved wood blocks. Lettering was then added to give the pertinent facts of time and place for each performance as it moved from town to town. The designs were probably colored by hand after the impressions were made, much as for the later Currier and Ives prints. The wood block illustrated (Figs. 89, 90), made for an early circus poster, shows a tightrope performer dressed in a patriotic costume of stars and stripes. In this print the color scheme would certainly have featured red, white and blue. There must have been many interesting woodblock designs for circus posters, but like the carved weathervane patterns they were generally discarded and destroyed when they had fulfilled their function of producing the pieces for which they were the intermediate stage. The unique block reproduced was preserved in perfect condition only because the rectangle of wood was utilized as the backing for a boxed ship model of the period, to which it is still attached.

For its main publicity the circus relied on the elaborately carved wagons which paraded to herald the show. A number of these circus wagons and details of the carvings which decorated them are reproduced and will be discussed. Before examining the circus-wagon and carrousel carvings, however, it will be worth pausing a moment to consider two personages whose combined talents brought into being much of this folk carving: Phineas T. Barnum, the great circus showman, and Samuel A. Robb, whom we have already mentioned in connection with trade signs, and who also specialized in the carving of circus-wagon figures and merry-go-round animals.

P. T. Barnum (1810–1891) was a Connecticut Yankee whose life history outdid the most fantastic Horatio Alger tales, and who became in his own time an American legend. He started his career as a peddler of molasses candy and cherry rum in his military training days; and at twenty-five he became a showman by buying and exhibiting Joice Heth, a negress alleged to be a hundred-and-sixty-one years old and to have been Washington's nurse. In the year 1836–37 he joined a traveling circus, organized a new company, bought a steamer, and took his circus to all the river towns down to New Orleans. In 1841 he bought the American Museum in New York. The following year he secured General Tom Thumb and some years later he imported Jenny Lind. In 1855 he started his "Great Asiatic Caravan, Museum and Menagerie," the pioneer of the super-circuses which were to flourish from that time on. In 1858 he toured the British Isles lecturing on "The Art of Money-Getting." In 1871 he organized the "Greatest Show on Earth" and when in 1887 he entered into partnership with Bailey, the Greatest Show became even greater.

The parade wagons made during the second half of the century for Barnum's circuses are a noteworthy part of our heritage. The circus carvings are entirely different from the unpretentious, utilitarian folk sculpture we find in other fields; they represent a native art indeed, but of a special kind, the popular art made for folk on holiday, with lavishness, gaiety and glitter the keynote of its style.

Samuel Robb's workshop at 195 Canal Street in New York turned out much of this early circus and carnival carving. Robb was an all-round carver to the American people in the third quarter of the nineteenth century; he carved patterns for weather-vanes, steamboat ornaments, and cigar-store and other trade sign figures, as well as all varieties of the circus and carrousel pieces which we are now considering. In the late seventies he was employed by the Sebastian Wagon Company of New York and during that period devoted all his energies to circus carving. At one time Barnum thought up the idea of having a group of life-size wooden figures representing nursery tale characters which would appear in his parades—Mother Goose, Cinderella, Bluebeard, Sindbad, and many others. Nearly all of these were made in Robb's shop, an order that must have kept things humming for quite a while. Robb was a fast, expert worker, individual in his technique in that he never used a mallet but drove the chisel with the palm of his hand. It seems that entire circus wagons, and the individual figures that adorned them, were occasionally redesigned and recarved to give them a new look; and it is likely that Robb took charge of such redecorating jobs as well as designing and executing countless circus-wagon figures and carvings of all kinds. Among the best pieces attributed to Robb are the Muses and monkeys reproduced (Figs. 95 & 96).

The old circus-wagons, of which only a small number have been preserved, represent American advertising art at its giddiest and gaudiest. The circus, as Barnum conceived it—and the other circus showmen followed suit as a matter of course—was heralded by magnificent, awe-inspiring wagons on parade. These wagons, rich with painted and gilded carving, dazzled the eyes of the spectators and caught their ears too, for some of them were bandwagons on the tops of which splendidly dressed musicians were seated in rows. The huge scale, lavish decoration, bright color and gilt, and lively sound of which a circus wagon was concocted were all intended to have a hypnotic effect on passers-by, to draw them irresistibly into the circus tents for the great show.

As we look more closely at a few of these circus-wagons, let us imagine away the cracks and peeling paint and the long-disused, static wheels. We must add in our mind's eye the prancing white horses in luxurious trappings which pulled the wagons slowly down the main streets, and the richly garbed drivers who cracked their long whips. We should listen too for the sprightly musicians who played the most popular, catchy tunes as the wagon rolled by followed by swarms of eager youngsters who skipped along with the parade as if they were led by the Pied Piper himself.

The bandwagon titled *United States* which is reproduced in Fig. 91 is probably the finest circus-wagon in existence. The central panel displays the Goddess of Liberty flanked by two Indians and surmounted by the American eagle. The background of the entire wagon is striped in red and white, with stars against a blue ground in the upper right. The gilded figures stand out in relief within the elaborate architectural framework, silhouetted against the background of stars and stripes. The wagon is a magnificent, super-scale American emblem. In its day, as its band played the *Star Spangled Banner,* it must have strongly appealed to the patriotic sentiments of the people as well as to their love of color and design.

The *Western Hemisphere* bandwagon (Fig. 94), no longer in existence, was extraordinarily designed in a rich, rococo arrangement which featured carved lions and elephants and national emblems. Quite different in type is the unusually chaste wagon (Fig. 92) whose nautical decoration of dolphins and Triton's spear is an outstanding piece of stylized folk art design.

The *Golden Age of Chivalry* (Fig. 93) is a striking circus-float wagon which was made for Barnum and Bailey by the Sebastian Wagon Company. It was designed by George Lawrence who worked for the Sebastians. The huge, muscular, two-headed dragon, carved in full round, was conceived as the protector of American womanhood. A gorgeously spangled young woman, undoubtedly of Mae West physique, was ensconced on the iron-railed seat between the dragon's wings, making a striking tableau as the wagon bowled along in parade.

The individual figures reproduced, all taken from one Barnum and Bailey circus-wagon (Figs. 95 & 96), were reputedly carved by Samuel Robb. Such figures, and a variety of others including a number of portraits of Jenny Lind, added a great deal of interest to the circus-wagons. The pair of huge monkeys are especially appealing, and seem much more human than the compactly designed and classically posed Muses. These figures are carved of pine, and were originally covered with gold leaf. It is not hard to imagine them glittering in the sun as their splendid wagon rolled majestically down Main Street.

The carrousel animals were in some ways very similar to the circus-wagon figures, being carved of soft wood and painted in much the same style. Both types of carving were designed in the carnival spirit. The circus figures were, however, planned to decorate the flat sides of the wagons and so their function was architectonic and their poses inevitably static. While some were carved in the round the backs were flattened to fit the wagon, and more often the circus-wagon carvings were executed in half-round or low relief. The carrousel animals were of course free-standing figures, carved in full round. As the merry-go-round was designed for exhilarating movement the most basic characteristic of the animals was their dynamic pose, intended to carry out and intensify the sense of motion of the revolving platform. The carrousel was a superanimated, life-size menagerie in wood, featuring the popular exotic circus creatures—lions, tigers, panthers, giraffes, ostriches, and fine white horses.

The huge painted rooster carved by a Vermont cabinet-maker (Fig. 99) is more prosaic than most carrousel subjects, but he struts along as only a carrousel rooster would. Every bit of him, from his shrewd, alert eye to the tip of his tail, adds to the conviction we feel from his muscular stride that we have here not a plain barnyard fowl but a feathered giant in seven-league boots.

The spirited white horse (Fig. 98) expresses high-powered speed in his sinewy legs, tensely arched neck and dilated nostrils, and especially in the finely stylized mane and tail that seem to lift with the rushing wind as he flies along. Young riders must have gripped the saddle and pulled the reins when they rode this large, mighty steed to be sure he would not gallop with them right off his platform. This carrousel horse, as is quite typical of the breed, is proportioned in such a way as to grow gradually larger toward the fore part, an abstract device designed to create the illusion of forward movement.

The merry-go-round horse has come to symbolize the American carnival spirit, and was featured in the recent musical comedy, *Carrousel*. There are few art forms in which the exuberance of a galloping horse is as vitally interpreted.

89. Miss America on a Tightrope

90. Rubbed Print from Wood Block

91.   "United States"

92.   Dolphin Circus Wagon

93. "The Golden Age of Chivalry"

94. "Western Hemisphere"

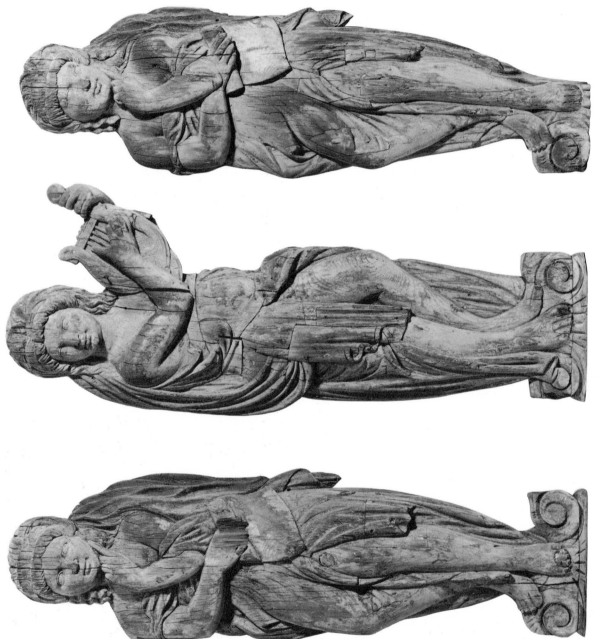

95. Muses from Circus Wagon

96.   Monkeys from Circus Wagon

97. Carrousel Panthers

98. Carrousel Horse

99. Carrousel Rooster

(Reproduced in color on front cover)

100.   Carrousel Giraffe

TOYS

ARLY AMERICAN TOYS, as we see them in the examples that have been preserved and in old children's portraits, are not as different as one might expect from our "educational playthings" of today. Modern block sets and streamlined wooden trains are deliberately reduced to essentials of design in accordance with conclusions reached by scientific studies of child psychology. The same thing was done instinctively by the makers of early toys. A fragment of a spotted toy cow from ancient Egypt is much like a primitive American toy dog, and both resemble the toy animals made today for use in progressive nursery schools. Children have always liked best the least intricate toys, that left most to their imaginations. The early homemade toys were so simply designed that their makers unconsciously achieved an almost abstract and highly individual style. That is why the old toys, whittled by the village carpenter, snipped out by a traveling tinsmith or baked by a local potter are collected today as worthy examples of native sculpture.

Children's portraits and paintings of family groups provide us with a glimpse of these toys in contemporary use. Toys were prominently displayed as a generic attribute of the child in provincial portraits, so that we have good painted records of the original appearance and approximate period of use of many early rattles, dolls, hobby-horses, toy wheelbarrows, carved animals, kites, and other playthings. In one primitive family portrait in watercolor owned by the author each of the children holds a different toy. In another, a likeness of a small Vermont boy painted on a coach panel about 1825 by one "Asahel Powers, Painter," there is a candle-stand in the center of which sits a fierce-looking gray dog mounted on a squeaking bellows. Squeak-toys have been seen in children's portraits painted as early as 1780 but most of them seem to date from the second and third quarters of the nineteenth century. A carved and painted wooden horse together with a mid-nineteenth-century daguerreotype showing a little boy who clutches that very horse in his hands as he sits for his likeness was recently found in Connecticut. An oil portrait of this period by Joseph Stock of a lad with a magnificent hobby-horse on wheels can be seen in the New-York Historical Society. The boy holds the horse's bridle in one hand, a whip in the other, and seems just ready to mount his fine steed. Dolls of many periods are to be found in children's portraits, and these are especially interesting when the paintings are dated. Such is the case in the delightful watercolor portrait of little Emma Clark with her doll, painted in 1829, which is in the Halladay-Thomas collection in Sheffield, Massachusetts.

Most toys worthy of consideration as folk art are of New England or Pennsylvania provenance. These two areas were the centers of the craft tradition in

America, and it can be seen from the list of plates that the majority of outstanding examples of folk art in all fields, as well as toys, have been found in Pennsylvania and New England.

The kinds of interesting folk toys produced during the eighteenth and nineteenth centuries in America make a long list. Among them are carved wooden dolls, jointed wood and metal "dancing" dolls and jumping toys, hobby-horses, wood and chalk animals, *papier mâché* squeak-toys, pottery bird whistles, and miniature decoys. There were also carved Gardens of Eden, Noah's Arks, and other "Sunday toys" whose Scriptural or educational value made them a permissible form of amusement when other playthings would have seemed too frivolous. The mechanical penny banks, while scarcely deserving of admission into the folk art category, were amusing and, we assume, character-building toys.

The doll and the hobby-horse were the most popular toys for the girl and boy of yesteryear, and large numbers of fine examples have been passed down from generation to generation. The eighteenth-century pine doll reproduced in Fig. 111 was made in New Hampshire about 1790. It is one of the oldest American dolls and one of the best from our point of view. Another delightful doll is the wooden—very wooden—Maine policeman with a removable hat (Fig. 101). The jointed Indian maid of Pennsylvania origin (Fig. 109) is especially attractive to us as a silhouette design, and must have been fun to play with for she will take any number of striking poses.

Hobby-horses are almost uniformly appealing, and are among the most forthright examples of folk carving. One now in the collection of Holger Cahill seems to have been carved by a chairmaker, for it stands on simple turned chair legs supported by stretchers. Another was made by the well-known ship carver Woodbury Gerrish at the Navy Yard in Portsmouth, New Hampshire (Fig. 104). Some late examples are stamped with the names of city companies, indicating that the making of hobby-horses had grown to large proportions by the end of the nineteenth century. The carved horses are characteristically plain and sturdy, with slightly curved bodies, simply carved heads and flat, conventionalized legs fastened to platforms on wheels or splaying out to meet wooden rockers. The coloring is often quite gay, some being spatter-painted or painted tan or gray or red overlaid with black swirls to suggest hair. Leather ears and real horse-hair tails were often attached and sometimes a forelock too. Leather and metal trappings and an upholstered carpet or even brocade seat were finishing touches to make some special hobbies super-luxurious. One mount was finished with a brass thumb-tack in the center of each round eye which gives the creature a wild, furious expression. Most hobby-horses appear to be placid and friendly, but some are arrogant and spirited, and it is extraordinary how convincingly the basic character of each horse is communicated by the carver, despite the conventionalized pose, expression and coloring.

The animated playthings were of a variety of kinds: articulated animals that jumped about when an attached stick was pushed or pulled, dolls that danced when jiggled on a string, hens that could be made to peck most realistically by raising and lowering a wooden ball which weighted the jointed heads and tails, miniature merry-go-rounds, Punch-and-Judy toys, and a number of others. The chalk animals that gently nod their socketed heads must have been among the most appealing toys for mild-mannered boys and girls.

Animal toys of painted *papier mâché* mounted on paper bellows that squeaked in supposedly appropriate but very slightly varied sounds, were made (and perished) in huge numbers. The survivors are generally worn and ragged, although a few splendid pieces such as the proud peacock (Fig. 107) seem scarcely touched. Some horrid mama must have snitched this one from the toy cupboard and placed it on her parlor mantel when it was still quite new.

Bird whistles, or blow birds as they used to be called, were another slightly noisy toy (Fig. 108). A breath blown into a hole in the tail emerged as a clear, high whistle from the back. These blow birds were made by eighteenth- and nineteenth-century English potters, and were widely imitated in the early nineteenth century, in much cruder form, in Ohio and Pennsylvania.

The quietest toys of all, known as "Sunday toys," were intended to be elevating as well as entertaining, and were reserved for Sundays when boisterous play was banned. Carved Gardens of Eden inhabited by Adam and Eve and the serpent were made for this purpose by the Pennsylvania whittler, Wilhelm Schimmel (Fig. 115). Noah's Arks, like the one which is now a part of the Essex Institute's fine collection of early toys (Fig. 119) were most popular. This was owned in her childhood by a Miss Willson, who was born in 1795. She said of it long ago that "it was made with the mind as well as with the hands," and that was the way it was meant to be played with too. The Ark contains more than fifty minutely carved and brilliantly enameled animals of all kinds and sizes, down to crickets, lady-bugs and butterflies. An article published in the magazine *Antiques* for July, 1931, describes a more primitive Noah's Ark carved in wood with all its passengers. This carving is attributed to an anonymous Negro bartender in the South, and is unique for the presence in the Ark of a man and woman with three offspring—a quite original interpretation of the beginnings of our population!

Other toys probably deemed sufficiently educational for Sunday use were the sets of carved wooden dolls engaged in various useful occupations. Such is the eighteenth-century group of jointed wooden dolls which operate miniature machines illustrating the processing of flax. These, of which the doll reproduced in Fig. 111 is one, are now in the collection of the South County Museum in Rhode Island. They are mounted on a wooden table and when a crank is turned several of the machines move in a lifelike manner. This pioneer mechanical toy includes beaters, swinging knives, spinning wheel, reel, loom, and several other devices. The sets of toy soldiers, carved in the early days in all sorts of characteristic attitudes, as well as the conventional upright pose, were probably banned on Sundays but used hard the rest of the week. A unique piece is an entire Civil War battlefield in miniature, owned by Mr. and Mrs. Rockwell Gardiner, which is realistically filled with carved soldiers and horses and cannons.

Children have always loved to create a toy microcosm of the grown-up life about them, and so a number of the customs, costumes, furnishings, and utensils of our ancestors are to be seen in miniature in early toys. When the itinerant tinsmith came by to fashion cooky cutters for mother, little daughters must have begged for a few for their doll households, and so a number of these miniatures are to be found today. One lady-shaped cooky cutter just an inch high is a cherished item in the important collection of Titus Geesey, a number of whose early toys are reproduced here. Among the rarest and most fetching of the miniature toys are the tiny decoys which were made in the late nineteenth century by decoy makers as toys for their children and grandchildren, as well as for display models. These minute ducks and swans were carved and painted with loving care, and must have been almost as much fun for the decoy makers to create as for the children to play with.

Carved animals of all varieties were among the most popular toys, and many of these deserve attention as prime examples of folk art. The carver's desire to make a toy that would be simple, sturdy, and immediately attractive to the child resulted in the production of delightful pieces of creative design like the small, mild-mannered horse, the strangely spotted dog with the painted chain collar, the genial whale (Figs. 103, 105, 118). A large wooden horse on wheels in the Essex Institute is of different pedigree—nothing funny or humble about this noble animal, of which examples have been found in a variety of sizes. This type of carved toy horse originated in the Austrian Tyrol and the American examples were most likely produced by a mid-nineteenth-century *émigré* woodcarver. He probably had several sons or other assistants working with him to have enabled him to produce the number of these carvings found to date, which are clearly the work of one shop. Hundreds of attractive animal toys are still to be found. Among these is the jointed dachshund (Fig. 106) and, most personable of all, numbers of carved and polychromed animal toys attributed to Wilhelm Schimmel (Figs. 112, 113, 114, 116, 117).

Schimmel is an almost legendary figure, for the story of his picturesque life was passed along by word of mouth but not set down in any written records in his lifetime and only the barest statistics and local anecdotes survive to tell his story. According to tradition this Pennsylvania German, who lived from 1817 to 1890, was wounded in the Civil War (some say the Mexican War), and from the late sixties to 1890 wandered about the Cumberland Valley near Carlisle, Pennsylvania, whittling toy birds, animals, and human figures for the village farmers' children, and occasional mantel ornaments for their elders. In this fashion he earned a meagre livelihood, or at least his board and lodging and the rum he is said to have liked too well. He often passed a carving across the bar in exchange for a pint, so that almost every tavern in the Cumberland Valley at one time had a Schimmel piece on display. During one prosperous period he is supposed to have traveled with a horse and buggy filled with carvings for sale, but mostly he carved his pieces as he went; and the children probably enjoyed watching saucy roosters and alert dogs emerge from a chunk of pine as much as they subsequently delighted in owning the finished toys. His only tools were a sharp jack-knife and bits of glass to smooth away the knife marks, and a few paint brushes. One can imagine the children staring, pop-eyed, as Schimmel whittled out the creature so vividly described in the Newark Museum's folk sculpture catalogue as "the little painted tiger with the great dog-like head, who fairly grins with the bliss of holding in his huge teeth a stiff and utterly helpless little man."

More than fifty years after his death the best authenticated facts and traditions about Schimmel were published, in some detail, in an article by Milton Flower in *Antiques*. According to Mr. Flower "Old Schimmel" was remembered as a big, somewhat terrifying, old man who sat by the roadside carving his figures. His rough voice, Germanic speech, peculiar habits, and purposeful wandering as a carver made him a noticeable character in his day. Greider's mill, near Carlisle, was home to Schimmel for some time, where John Greider, a miller and farmer, gave him lodging in the loft of his washhouse. Here, by a covered bridge, Schimmel was well-remembered as a raw-boned, ugly man who sat for hours, carving and singing in German. When he was not at Greider's any hayloft or cellar was his shelter, and he is said often to have had free lodging in the county jails. Schimmel died in an almshouse at Carlisle at the age of seventy-three, and was buried in the potter's field. Only one brief notice of his death was published, in a Carlisle newspaper: " 'Old Schimmel' the German who for many years tramped through this and adjoining counties, making his headquarters in jails and almshouses, died at the Almshouse on Sunday. His only occupation was carving heads of animals out of soft Pine wood. These he would sell for a few pennies each. He was apparently a man of a very surly disposition."

Helen McKearin, discussing Schimmel in an article written for the *New York Sun,* points out that the now famous Schimmel eagles, like the vagabond carver himself, seem to have a restless, roaming nature. Certainly there is a free, virile look to all these carvings which were crudely whittled and painted in strong, elemental colors—black, gray, red, yellow, and green. The subjects include animals of many kinds: dogs, lions, tigers, squirrels, parrots, roosters, eagles, small birds, and also a few Hessian soldiers and conventionalized fruit pieces. There have also been found some sheep with real wool glued to their wooden hides, and in his last months Schimmel is said to have carved a small portrayal of the Crucifixion. Rarest of all is the entire Garden of Eden (Fig. 115) with Adam and Eve and the serpent in the tree, all nailed to a picket-fenced board. One of Schimmel's Adam and Eve groups was exhibited at the Cumberland County Fair in the 1880's and he hurled curses at the judges who failed to award him a ribbon.

It has been estimated that four or five hundred of these animal and figure carvings, executed in the tradition of German peasant art, were made during the last twenty-five years of Schimmel's life. Other "Pennsylvania pine" carvings are more finished and graceful, but the Schimmel figures are unique for the primitive vitality of conception and execution that makes the smallest of the pieces a major example of folk art design.

It is interesting to find that toymakers like Schimmel ended up by carving household ornaments that were cherished as works of art in their day as well as in ours (see Fig. 141). Schimmel's toy eagles grew in stature as he carved his way through the Cumberland Valley until, attaining a three-foot wingspread, they were considered suitable decorations for the parlor mantel and the garden flagpole. Today they occupy places of honor in the folk art collections of our leading museums.

102. Balancing Toy

101. Toy Policeman

103.   Toy Horse

104.   Hobby Horse

105.　Toy Dog

106.　Jointed Dachshund Toy

107. Peacock Squeak-Toy

108. Goose Whistle

109. Jointed Indian Doll

110. Revolutionary Soldier

111. Doll

112, 113, 114.   Schimmel Toys

115.   Garden of Eden

118. Toy Whale

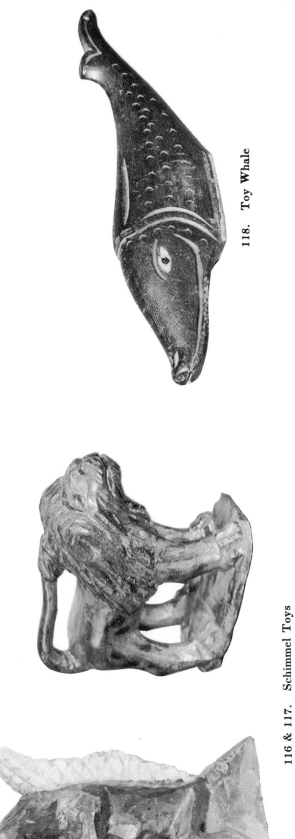

116 & 117. Schimmel Toys

119. Noah's Ark

DECOYS

THE MAKING OF DECOYS is one of our few indigenous crafts, having been originated by the Indians long before the arrival of the white man. The word "decoy" was used abroad to describe the traps into which wild fowl were enticed, and the tame birds which were used to lead them into these snares. It was in America, however, that artificial birds were first set up to attract wild fowl within range of a concealed hunter.

Most fields of interest have been written up by numerous people, but the investigation of the decoy has remained a one-man achievement. Joel Barber formed a large collection of decoys and wrote a book about them in 1932, and since that time nothing has been published on this subject that is not directly indebted to his first researches. Mr. Barber is still actively interested in the hobby to which he has devoted a full quarter of a century. He has discussed some of his recent thoughts about decoys with this author, and his book forms the basis for the summary here given of the history of decoy making. The difference between Mr. Barber's approach to the subject and ours is that he is interested in decoys from the point of view of the practical sportsman; we, however, are primarily concerned with them because, though designed for purely utilitarian purposes, their makers incidentally created bird carvings which merit consideration as folk art.

The American Indian bird lures were the first decoys. The earliest were crudely shaped mud heaps or bunches of dried grass fastened to sticks which roughly simulated bird forms. These temporary figures were succeeded by the first true decoys which were of two kinds: stuffed skins and birds made of bullrushes painted in natural colors. These aboriginal decoys had been made by a long-extinct tribe of Indians, the predecessors of the Paiutes. Perfectly preserved examples of them were discovered during the excavations of Lovelock Cave in Nevada, conducted for the Museum of the American Indian in New York, where these decoys, one of which is here illustrated (Fig. 120), may be seen.

From such primitive beginnings the making of artificial birds developed rapidly, for the Colonists imitated the Indian lures, and subsequently decoy making was taken up in Europe as well. Scores of varieties of decoys can now be identified, about evenly divided between floating decoys used to lure water birds and stick-up decoys for shore birds.

Decoy making is one of the few forms of our folk art expression that has survived the machine age for, though in the latter part of the nineteenth century factories produced decoys in quantity, the home-carved varieties have remained more popular with discriminating gunners throughout the country, and are still being made by hunters, carpenters, village whittlers, and professional decoy makers wherever there is bird hunting. Decoy making, moreover, continues as a modern craft based very closely on the methods of earlier generations of decoy carvers. Perhaps during our time a radically new kind of decoy made of some light, durable plastic will be perfected, but to this date, though plastic decoys have been experimented with, decoy making remains an old-fashioned craft.

The techniques and materials of decoy making are widely varied. The main types of decoys are: those carved of solid blocks of white pine or cedar; flat wood stick-up profiles; those made of cork and balsa wood; hollow decoys built up of several pieces of wood hollowed out and fastened together; decoys made of slats nailed together; factory-made wooden decoys turned on a reproducing lathe, with heads and tails finished by hand; folding tin snipe, patented in 1874, of pressed tin made in two halves, hinged at the top and fastened together on a stick when in use. The cork, balsa wood, hollow, slat, factory-turned, and tin decoys were later developments and are inferior in design to the earlier types of carved floating and stick-up decoys which we illustrate in this chapter as valid examples of folk sculpture.

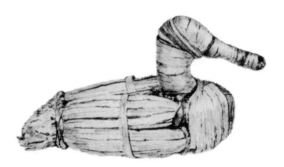

120.   Aboriginal Canvas-back Decoy

The carved wood decoy, an example of which is here shown in profile, front and top view (Fig. 121), is the most important type both for sportsmen and collectors of folk art. In this category are to be found likenesses of every species of water fowl which is hunted with decoys. The method of making these carved decoys, which originated in Colonial times, was perfected about the Civil War era and has continued in use with virtually no changes to this day. Decoy making, as Mr. Barber describes it, consists of four separate processes: body making, head making, assembling, and painting; with the supplementary minor operation of rigging which consists of attaching the necessary weights and anchors. The decoy maker first cuts the wood for a number of bodies into the required lengths and hews them roughly into the desired shape with a carpenter's hatchet on a chopping block. Next the hewn bodies are placed one by one in a vise and finished with a long, narrow-bladed drawknife. The heads are made in similar fashion, being sawed rather than hewn out of the small pieces of wood, usually according to a pattern or template. The heads are then finished like the bodies, and final touches are usually whittled with a jack-knife. The heads and bodies are next assembled, the heads being attached with long iron spikes and supplementary nailing. The decoys are then sandpapered to remove tool marks, and finally painted. Occasionally glass or tack eyes are added, or the eyes may be indicated by incised carving instead of merely being painted in. The chief difference between old and modern decoy making lies in the painting, for some contemporary craftsmen have developed realistic feather painting while in the past formalized patterns of solid color were the rule.

Mr. Barber's book devotes a chapter to "Regional Decoys," with descriptions

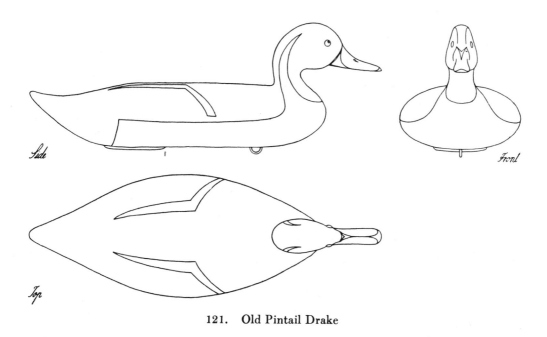

121.   Old Pintail Drake

of those characteristic of Nova Scotia, New England, Long Island, Barnegat, the Chesapeake, Back Bay, Currituck Sound, and the Gulf states. It is fascinating to read how the different kinds of decoys are used in hunting the various wild fowl represented, and to see how many types of decoys might be assembled by a collector.

Decoys, for a number of reasons, make an especially pleasing collectors' hobby. First, of course, the carved wild fowl are interesting and attractive and so worth collecting and preserving. There is a wide variety obtainable, and almost all of them were once made in such quantities that good specimens can still be had at reasonable prices. The pieces are moderate in size, and can be nicely displayed. Mr. Barber's collection includes examples of every interesting type of decoy, and he effectively designed a series of shallow shelves set against white walls for their display.

If anyone feels at all inclined to consider collecting decoys, his book will crystallize the decision, for it is, as well as a painstaking history and practical handbook, a delightful omnibus of collector's anecdotes. A rare whistling swan was found in the granary loft of a farm on the eastern shore of Maryland, and we share

in retrospect the collector's thrill when he spotted it among a group of broken
derelict decoys thrown in a heap as discarded equipment. A characteristic tale of
his search concerns a unique specimen of a sea loon made by a Maine lighthouse
tender (Fig. 128). Mr. Barber tells how one Captain Rand secured the old decoy,
presented it to him, and told him how the decoy was used to snag a loon and finally
how the loon was cooked:

> "To cook a loon," says Captain Rand, "they parboil first and use some sort of 'chemical,'
> then they roast it."
>
> Impressed by the word "chemical," the writer ventured the question—"Soda?"
>
> "Maybe 'twas," said the Captain, "but if they are cooking loon for me, I'd specify Dutch
> Cleanser."

This loon is a perfect specimen of a collectors' item that combines just about
every desirable attribute—top quality and condition, scarcity, and even a flavorful
story associated with its acquisition. It is in fact one of the outstanding American
bird carvings, regardless of category. The long, flat shape and black-and-white
pattern were dictated by its practical function as a decoy; but its maker, though
he did not do so deliberately, created a carved form any modern sculptor would be
proud to claim. This is true, in varying degrees, of all the decoys we have chosen
to illustrate. These decoys are made in the basic forms of the birds they were intended to lure, but they are far from literal copies. Made with the simplest tools,
the decoys were executed with the non-realistic attitude on the part of the maker
that characterizes all primitive and abstract art in which design predominates. This
is the chief reason that they have been admired by modern artists. The old decoys
are so formalized as to have an almost twentieth-century air, and examples like
the primitive blue heron and the black plover (Figs. 126 & 127) have been compared
to the forms of Mestrovic and other modern sculptors. The most interesting part
of all this is that the abstraction, in decoy making, was entirely deliberate on the
part of the early carvers, who had somehow come to the conclusion that literal
reproductions did not attract the birds as effectively as decoys created as abstract
symbols.

It is extraordinary how vitally the essential character of the bird is suggested,
in distilled essence, by the simplest plastic means. This heightening of basic at-
tributes was found to be practically effective in decoy making, and distinguishes
the best sculpture of all kinds. The loon (Fig. 129) has a body like a flat-iron and
an unrealistic notched silver tail, but its turned neck, made of a gnarled root, gives
it a quick, bright look that exaggerates the alert quality of this bird and makes it
seem livelier than any realistic model could. The beautifully shaped pintail drake
(Fig. 123) is the very type of smooth-swimming water fowl, and its drastically sim-
plified feather design must have been clearly visible to the game ducks at quite a
distance. This decoy's surface design with its contrasts of straight and curved
lines and interesting tonal pattern makes as satisfying an abstract arrangement as
a modernist's "Composition." The male eider duck (Fig. 122) is a similar abstraction, in an even bolder pattern. We can imagine the mates being irresistibly drawn
to so vigorous an impression of one of their kind, resting quietly on the water, and
our eye is equally held by the fine, strong form and design of this decoy. The deli-
cately accented curves of the elegant wild swan and the exaggerated bulk and

squareness of the oversized Canada goose (Figs. 124 & 130) are good examples of the old decoy makers' highly stylized versions of the fowl they aimed to attract.

Mr. Barber reproduces a modern representation of a Canada goose decoy made in the nineteen-thirties, which is realistically shaped and elaborately painted in a good imitation of the actual appearance of the feathers. In looking from our roughly blocked out and simply finished goose to this sleek modern specimen there is one immediate reaction: namely that the old decoy creates a much stronger impression. It appears somehow more solid, for the eye takes in the whole mass as a unit, while it skims over the elaborately painted surface of the modern decoy. The latter makes a more diffused impression, for the eye tends to pick out details here and there—feathers, a beak, tail, wings—rather than to assimilate at a glance the whole compact goose form with its suggestion of latent movement. This, it seems likely, is also the difference between the way the two decoys would impress a goose; and certainly accounts for the attitude of the old decoy carver, who reduced his forms and surfaces to their basic essentials in order to create the most instantaneous and concentrated impression on his quarry. Needless to remark, the same differential accounts for our selection of the old decoy as an interesting example of folk art. It seems as if we might safely formulate a positive conclusion on which to base decoy making, and decoy collecting: it is the simplest and most stylized decoys that most strongly attract both the wild fowl and the decoy collector!

122. Male Eider Duck

123. Pintail Drake

124. Wild Swan

125. Loon

126.   Shore Birds

127.   Plover

128.   Sea Loon

129.   Loon

130.   Canada Goose

SCULPTURE FOR HOUSE AND GARDEN

THE EARLY AMERICAN HOUSE has been one of the most popular models for modern interior decoration. Yet in most contemporary adaptations there is little feeling for the rich color and design that animated the homes of our ancestors. Department-store versions of Americana have dominated popular taste with their stock furniture of orange-shellacked pine and maple, knotty pine walls, white muslin curtains, and glossy white woodwork. Actually, the typical early American interior was entirely different from the emasculated popular version. Woodwork and paneling were often elaborately carved and painted in a variety of strong colors. Floors might be stenciled in gay repeat designs, and plaster walls, frequently tinted in pastel shades, were sometimes painted with bright stenciled or freehand scenes. Fabrics were of various weaves and designs, typically dyed in vivid colors rather than bleached to white. We are especially interested in the fact that every household was further embellished not only with prints and paintings that hung on the walls, but with all varieties of sculptural decoration.

A good restoration of a typical early American house might well include a few ornamental pieces of carved wood or whalebone, or perhaps a group of pottery or plaster figures, and decorative accessories such as doorstops and andirons. Some architectural carving, functionally designed for interior or exterior, would be a correct detail. Even the homely objects of daily use in the kitchen could provide many attractive examples of early American design. And in the garden might be displayed a few interesting pieces of folk sculpture in the form of lawn or fountain figures.

From the late eighteenth through the latter part of the nineteenth century folk art flourished in America. The people wanted their surroundings to be beautiful as well as practical, and they had the conviction that anyone who wished to could paint or carve. It was this democratic and typically American attitude toward the arts, combined with a vigorous and uninhibited sense of design, which caused the production of the large body of native folk art.

Though most folk sculptures were designed for use, with decoration as a secondary object, a number of household ornaments were made simply for the pleasure of producing and enjoying them. Decorative carvings are the most interesting pieces in this category. Carved mantel ornaments such as a pair of polychromed pheasants in the Williamsburg collection are typical but relatively conventional. Elaborately whittled display pieces in patriotic vein like the figure of Liberty and the alert little George Washington on horseback are representative examples of folk sculpture at its best (Figs. 153 & 156). Carved statuettes of domesticated animals were especially popular in their time, for the rural household was closely tied up with the livestock of the farm. These modest animal carvings are now eagerly sought by collectors (see Fig. 151). A "Venus de Milo" with a strange, archaic smile, a piece that defies classification, was whittled by the Pennsylvanian, Aaron Mounts. Mounts, said to have been an admirer of Schimmel's carvings, also brought into being the amazing poodle and the delightful little owl shown in Figs. 140 & 144. Among the most naïve decorative carvings are various scenes, rendered in the round and in low relief and appropriately painted. There are a number of examples of hunting groups, with a huntsman and one or more dogs, of which Fig. 155 is a delightful example. A whole barnyard scene whittled in scale to fit into a cigar box is owned by the Newark Museum. There is a large carved view of New Amsterdam in the Rudolph Haffenreffer collection that must have been designed to be hung as a featured parlor ornament. Among the story-telling relief scenes one in the Harden de V. Pratt collection represents Molly Pitcher of Revolutionary fame loading a cannon against a background crammed with British and American soldiers. Another, an exciting fight between a frontiersman and an Indian in the collection of Mrs. Beryl De Mott, is captioned "Bronco Charlie, His Last Shot."

Glazed pottery representations of animals and people were common household ornaments during the eighteenth and early nineteenth centuries. Some of these pieces were imported from English, French and German potteries, but more were made at home (see Figs. 145 & 157).

In the second half of the nineteenth century plaster "cottage ornaments" outstripped the pottery products in popularity. The making of chalkware in this country goes back at least to 1768 when one Henry Christian Geyer advertised in Boston that he practiced the "Art of Fuser Simulacrorum or making of all sorts of curious animals of Plaster of Paris." It is, however, the late Pennsylvania rather than the early New England chalkware that collectors know so well today. This minor sculptural art flourished in the second half of the nineteenth century on a scale comparable to the print production of Messrs. Currier and Ives. A type of household decoration that closely paralleled in subject matter and style the Currier and Ives prints was the "statuary" executed in the 1870's in New York by John Rogers. Titles of the pieces, priced from ten to fifty dollars, included "Playing Doctor," "Weighing the Baby," "Going for the Cows," "Country Post Office," and "The Council of War." These Rogers groups, realistic castings of a wide variety of genre subjects, cannot be classified as folk art (or art of any kind), but as household ornaments popular for a number of years they played a part in the life of the people and as such are worthy of our interest.

Chalkware, made largely by the Germans of Pennsylvania, but also found in sections of New England settled by Germans, was the cheapest available form of household ornament. Almost all of it was made between 1850 and 1885. Many pieces sold, generally via the itinerant peddlers, for as little as fifteen cents (see Fig. 137), and averaged no more than half a dollar for the more elaborate items. Chalkware was for the provincial middle classes a substitute for the Staffordshire owned by the wealthy, and the chalk pieces generally followed popular Staffordshire models. The English designs were, however, infused with a German folk art flavor, and developed in America with bolder patterns and simpler color. The chalk pieces were brighter, sturdier, and both literally and figuratively lacked the polish of the aristocratic Staffordshire porcelains. The animals and people all have a friendlier, less arrogant pose and expression, as if adapting themselves to the environment of ordinary folk, where they would grace tables of scrubbed pine rather than polished mahogany.

The subjects to be found in chalkware cover a wide range. There are all kinds of wild and domesticated animals: squirrels, cats, dogs, roosters, deer (Fig. 137). We find formalized fruit pieces and horns of plenty, and Christmasy churches and angels and Kris Kringles (Fig. 139). There are bloomer girls inspired by a Currier and Ives print and other figures of various kinds, some pastoral, a few as prosaic as the fireman (Fig. 138).

Our concern with chalkware as a folk art is due to the interesting stylization which is its chief quality. The simplification of form and gay, abstract patterning of vivid color on the white ground makes these pieces look strikingly modern.

Scrimshaw, unlike chalkware, was a decorative art wholly native to America, and specifically to New England. This work, mentioned in *Moby Dick* as "scrimshander," was whalebone carving, in the round or incised, made aboard ship on whaling voyages. The substance used was scraps of whalebone or whales' teeth. The implements were ordinary jack-knives and saws for carving, gimlets made of nails for drilling holes, files and grindstones and wood ashes for finishing, and sail makers' needles for incising. With these primitive materials whalemen contrived wonderful carvings to be brought ashore as gifts for their stay-at-home families and friends. They made busks decorated with scenes elaborately engraved and colored with India inks, intricate swifts for winding yarn, magnificently decorated jagging wheels for crimping pie crust, chessmen and cribbage boards, and canes topped with walrus heads or plump ladies' legs. Besides the countless varieties of useful pieces there were scrimshaw pictures of ship and whaling scenes, patriotic subjects, and sentimental and everyday scenes of all kinds, incised and inked on pieces of flattened whalebone and on whales' teeth. The carving reproduced as Fig. 147 is an extraordinary piece of sculpture in the round made from the teeth of whales by an anonymous tar. One can imagine his having painstakingly carved out this scrimshaw proposal for his lady-love during long years at sea, to present to her in lieu of a verbal proposal on his return from the voyage.

Scrimshaw pieces were a characteristic household decoration in the towns of New Bedford and Nantucket and others which played a part in the whaling industry. Decorative accessories common to almost every early American home were doorstops of pottery, metal or wood (Figs. 135 & 150), andirons, perhaps in the form of Indians, George Washingtons or Hessian soldiers, and bootjacks shaped in some interesting form such as a naked lady or a devil (Fig. 134).

The early kitchen was a veritable treasure-room for decorative objects of daily use, and the Pennsylvania kitchen was especially rich in utilitarian folk art. Here one might find a carved stone pig used to weigh down the top of a barrel of sauerkraut; there were always arrays of tin cooky cutters and pudding molds and carved butter and cake molds; and there was almost certainly an iron jamb stove with interesting decoration on the plates.

The love of rich design was everywhere apparent. The housewife was not content to serve her butter or cookies in unadorned squares or circles. Her sets of carved molds enabled her to stamp butter with the patterns of swans, eagles, cows, tulips, hearts, or any number of designs (Fig. 160). Her cooky cutters made it possible to bake cookies in all kinds of interesting shapes—roosters, horses, squir- rels, rabbits, men and women, Indians, or even a William Penn or Uncle Sam. It must have been a red-letter day for the *hausfrau* when the itinerant tinsmith came by with his jingling cart and made her some newly designed cooky cutter, while the whole family watched his nimble fingers at work with shears and solder.

The carved *marzipan* and *springerle* cake molds made it possible for thin Christmas and Easter cakes to be stamped in low-relief designs. The hard-wood *springerle* boards were carved in intaglio, most often in composite groups of two to twelve patterns enclosed in separate squares, to mark the cutting lines for small individual cakes; while the *marzipan* boards were often designed for a single large cake as in the splendid example reproduced (Fig. 159). The dough was rolled thin, laid on the mold and pressed, so that the details of the design would appear in re- lief. This cake dough rose scarcely at all in the baking, so the designs remained sharp. The finished cakes could be kept for months and, though they were so hard that it has been said it was as easy to eat the board as the cake, they were evidently a popular delicacy. *Springerle* cakes were most often baked for Easter; *marzipan* cakes and all kinds of cookies for Christmas. Both cookies and cakes could be fur- ther ornamented with colored frosting or a sprinkling of colored sugar, and must have made a splendid display at festive seasons. Even pie crusts were often stamped with decorative designs for special occasions, and the round pie molds that have been preserved are attractive examples of carved design.

While cooky cutters and butter and cake molds are collected today as folk art, they must be relegated to a minor category. The stove plates preserved from the early five-jamb stoves (Figs. 161–164) and the contemporary iron fire-backs (Fig. 165) are relics of major importance, for they represent the outstanding examples of low-relief sculpture in metal produced in this country. Due to the efforts of Henry Chapman Mercer a large number of the best plates were rescued from junk heaps in the first years of our century and preserved as a unique collection which can now be viewed in the Bucks County Historical Society. Good examples are to be found in a number of other museums as well.

The early cast-iron stove, about two feet square, made of five plates fitted to- gether, was usually connected with the jamb of the kitchen fireplace, from which hot embers could be shoveled into the stove. Jamb stoves were made from the sec- ond through the third quarters of the eighteenth century, but most of the best ex- amples date between 1740 and 1765. The stoves were local to the communities settled by Germans, chiefly in eastern Pennsylvania, but also in New Jersey, New York and Virginia. Many of the best plates were made at Durham Furnace in Bucks County, Warwick Furnace in Chester County, Stiegel's Elizabeth Furnace in Lan- caster County, and Marlboro Furnace in the Shenandoah Valley .

Most of the plates are anonymous, though some of them have names lettered within the design. Stiegel's is the most famous name to be found on a stove-plate, and many of the best plates made at Elizabeth Furnace were designed by him. "Baron" Heinrich Wilhelm Stiegel had founded the town of Manheim in 1762. He operated a glass works there, and Stiegel glass is as well known to collectors throughout the country now as it was in Manheim in the eighteenth century. Iron was Stiegel's first venture in the business world, and he amassed a considerable fortune in Elizabeth Furnace and Channing Forge, where he designed and had cast numerous ornamental stove-plates, one of which is reproduced (Fig. 164).

The front and two side plates of the stoves were decorated, the largest number with Biblical scenes, some with allegorical or genre subjects or stylized designs. The Biblical scenes, with quoted text, were meant to serve as object lessons to the householders while they enjoyed the cosy heat of the stove, and Mercer's book on stove-plates was well named *The Bible in Iron*. One typical genre scene recording a family quarrel is accompanied by a rhymed sermon on patience. The decorated stove, which was the most prominent object in the kitchen, was indeed a three-dimensional household sermon. These stoves bear concrete witness to the deeply moral and religious nature of the Pennsylvania Germans.

Many of the stove-plates and the iron fire-backs which were cast in similar designs are very beautiful, with soundly designed scenes, detailed with childlike directness through strong outlines and expressive gestures. The interpretation is vigorous, often dramatic or humorous, and the elements of the design are almost uniformly well composed.

The "Wedding Fable" (Fig. 161) is a good example. This scene is generally interpreted as an old folklore custom of a test to determine which maiden will first secure a husband. A pair of breeches hangs from the lowest branch of a leafy tree, barely within reach of three maidens who seem to be trying to pull them down with forked sticks. At the other side of the tree the husband-elect claps his hands to spur on the competition. The figures, tree, bit of ground, and stylized clouds are placed within the rectangular frame, so that there is no overlapping, allowing forms and action to be presented with maximum clarity. The profiling of the actors points up their gestures and gives them rhythmic continuity as a series of related silhouettes. The foliated scroll at the bottom serves as a decorative base for the scene.

The scenes are all well coordinated with the architectonic framework within which they are placed, or with the ornamental scrollwork which accompanies them. A few like "The Plow" (Fig. 163) and some of the floral designs are almost purely abstract, conceived in terms of crisp, linear pattern.

These stove-plates are evidence of a strong survival of the peasant folk art of Germany, and of the fresh re-interpretation along simpler and bolder lines of an Old World art on American soil.

Sculpture in low relief is seen in another medium in the carvings which ornament the interior and exterior woodwork of numbers of fine early houses in every part of the country, and especially along the eastern seaboard where ship carvers practiced their trade. Undoubtedly the most famous house decorator was Samuel McIntire, the "master carver of Salem," who ornamented scores of homes and public buildings in his town around 1800. Although much of McIntire's carving is, like that of his contemporary Rush, more finished than the pieces we classify as folk art, his style was based on highly developed craftsmanship rather than academic training, and many of his decorative sculptures are so original and native in inspiration that they may logically be included as within the folk art tradition. Among these are a number of mantels ornamented with vigorously carved eagles, a set of interesting architectural panels which were placed over the windows of

Hamilton Hall, a large, bold eagle carved in low relief for the doorway of the old Customs House, and one in the round for the City Hall. One of his most remarkable pieces of sculpture is the coat of arms of Massachusetts carved in a lunette for the pediment of the gate of Salem Common (Fig. 168).

131.   Hatch's Sign

Simeon Skillin was another eighteenth-century house carver, best known for his ship carving but also for his fine furniture and the figures which he executed for Boston and Salem doorways.

Just about a hundred years after Skillin and McIntire ornamented the houses of Boston and Salem with their carvings, a retired maritime carver by the name of Edbury Hatch was actively at work decorating the houses of Newcastle and Damariscotta in Maine. The brief summary of his life and work which follows is based on an unpublished manuscript by Samuel Green.

Hatch was born in Newcastle in 1849 and died there in 1935. As a youth he apprenticed himself in his native town to William Southwork, a successful ship carver. Later he was employed by Colonel Sampson in Bath, where he helped to carve a number of Sampson's famous figureheads. During the following years he himself executed figureheads for a number of ships. In the eighties, with the decline of shipping, he was forced to accept employment as a night watchman in Charlestown, Massachusetts. In the nineties he returned to Newcastle where he developed the early ship carving for which he had been trained into an original and lively kind of architectural ornament.

Hatch's architectural work enriched the modest frame houses of Newcastle and Damariscotta. A good deal of it, comprising a large and remarkable series of carvings, is still in place. The most varied assortment of carved ornamentation was executed for his own house in Newcastle, just "for the joy of the work," as a local newspaper put it. The exterior carvings ornamented a portico for the front door and canopies for two ell doors, and included a fantastic gutter spout in the form of a gargoyle that looks quite a bit like a billethead, and a State of Maine Seal (Fig. 167). The interior of Hatch's house was also filled with carvings—eagles on a cannon, a tree full of cats, a panel of gilded fishes, and a chest decorated with sailing ships tacking out of a rocky harbor. Only the latter two have survived, but all the exterior ornament was preserved when it was ripped off the house. It has been set up again on the Maine houses of Mr. and Mrs. Henry Beston at Nobleboro and of Mrs. John Cunningham at Wiscasset. The front door portico, now on the Cunningham house, consists of a carved cornice topped by a flying dove with side lattices of a highly stylized grapevine design. Two panels in the railing area represent a hunting dog stalking some unseen prey, with a bird, butterfly and bee flying overhead; also a bear foraging for nuts, accompanied by an enormous dragon-fly. The doorways of the ells are owned by the Bestons. One has a pair of fantastic side supports made up of the heads of lions and foxes, joined by serpents and topped by a pair of gigantic tassels, over which is a pediment filled with a rich variety of fruits and vegetables. The other ell door canopy is composed of an ornate console supporting a foliated pediment, where a frieze of large-leafed foliage converges at the center on a woman's head. This was carved in full round and is definitely reminiscent of a sternboard portrait on a ship. The State of Maine Seal formerly over the end ell door is a vitalized version of the conventional design. In this piece, as in all of Hatch's carvings, a varied relief allows the play of sunlight over the surface to animate the design with strong tonal contrasts.

Another striking piece of work by Hatch, still preserved in Newcastle, is a carved and painted emblem for the doorway of the Taniscot Fire Company, which features a fireman's hat surrounded by the fire-house bucket, rope, lantern, ladder, hatchet, hose, and bugle horn. A number of front door portals and a summerhouse, carved with robust, stylized foliage and grapevine motifs, are still preserved in Newcastle and Damariscotta.

Hatch possessed a hundred tools, most of which he had made himself, and his style was self-made too. He owned a couple of drawings of modestly draped nudes cut from an old newspaper, labeled "a perfect man's proportions" and "a perfect woman's proportions" but, aside from these models, which one suspects were largely ignored, and his craft training as a ship carver, he was self-taught. He relied, boldly and with splendid results, on his own liking for rich, lively, well balanced design. Hatch's sculpture was executed with great gusto in a tangy, clean-cut Maine idiom. His best work, done in the last decade of the nineteenth century, represents the last flowering of the fine tradition of underivative New England woodcarving which originated with the early native figurehead carvers.

Besides the carved decoration which adorned architectural woodwork, a few exterior ornaments of wood and cast iron should be noted. An interesting decoration made for a barn near Portland, Maine, is a gargoyle waterspout carved in the

132. Timothy Dexter House

form of a highly stylized cat's head. This piece is thought to have been made by a ship carver, according to information secured when it was recorded by the Index of American Design. A number of painted iron pigeons have been found in Pennsylvania which are said to have served as ornaments for houses and fences, and around 1900 the snow-catcher eagles were common roof ornaments almost everywhere. Among the most fascinating exterior ornaments are small iron Indians, cast in low-relief profiles, an example of which is displayed in the first Pennsylvania room in the American Wing of the Metropolitan Museum. These were said to have been attached during the eighteenth century to the doors of houses whose land was purchased from the Indians, as a protective sign to prevent destruction by Indians who might assume the land was rightly theirs.

The lawns and gardens of American houses were from early times considered an appropriate setting for sculpture of various sorts. About the most extraordinary landscape decorations ever conceived were the life-size figures of famous men executed by Joseph Wilson the ship carver (probably with shop assistants) for "Lord" Timothy Dexter of Newburyport. Timothy Dexter (1748–1806) was an illiterate but shrewd Yankee trader who made a fortune during and after the Revolution, and who in middle life became obsessed with his own importance to a degree bordering on madness. He took the title of "Lord" and had his own poet laureate, bought a mansion on High Street in Newburyport, which is still standing, and converted his estate into a "Museum" by commissioning over fifty wooden figures to be set upon rows of pillars and triumphal arches which dotted the grounds.

In front of the mansion (Fig. 132) were thirteen five-foot pillars in a straight row, one for each state, on which the great figures of history were placed. The three presidents, Washington, Adams and Jefferson, were set immediately in front of the entrance. Benjamin Franklin, John Hancock, Alexander Hamilton, Rufus King, and John Jay were placed nearby. Elsewhere, to quote Dexter's description in *A Pickel for the Knowing Ones,* were "2 grenedears on the top of the hous, 4 Lions below, 1 Eagle, is in the Coupolow. . . . One Younecorne, one Dogg, Addam and Eave in the garden,—one horse," and, he adds, "The houll is not concluded on as yet." Additions included Bonaparte, Lord Nelson, Louis XVI, Venus, the great Indian Cornplanter, a strolling preacher and many others, with a carved portrait of the eccentric "Lord" himself near the front gate, on a pedestal on which was inscribed "I am the first in the East."

The entire plan was for a sort of huge Peaceable Kingdom in sculpture, with the great statesmen and men of letters and science from all parts of the world, Biblical characters, lions and a lamb, and other animals. The whole scheme signified, as J. P. Marquand interprets it in his book on Dexter, "the unity of nations and the great concord of the earth." Of all this, almost nothing has survived. There is preserved a lone figure of William Pitt (Fig. 154) which sold at auction for a dollar after Dexter's death, the eagle on the cupola which is still in its original place, a pair of stylized female figures carved in low relief that were originally set on either side of an arch, and a few dismembered arms and legs.

The ordinary horse-head hitching posts and hitching-post figures, flagpole ornaments and garden statues seem tame decorations compared with Timothy Dexter's colossal sculptural scheme. However, these common species of yard ornaments were all representative examples of folk art. A few are of unusual interest, such as the wooden hitching-post heads in the form of grotesque caricatures, and a few are of extraordinary quality (Figs. 143 & 146).

A unique New England object is the carved gate made about 1850 by one Hobart Victory Wilton for his front yard in Waterbury, Connecticut (Fig. 166).

The carved and painted mermaid (Fig. 133) is another unique piece of sculpture. It served, probably in the first years of the nineteenth century, as a fountain figure in a Baltimore garden. A metal tube ran up the body to the mouth, allowing the mermaid to spout water which must have risen and fallen in a curve, repeating in reverse the lines of her sweeping tail. The contours and coloring of this lithe little mermaid are simple in the extreme. Her silhouette is nothing more than a sturdy, undulating line. She is colored a flesh pink and two shades of green—sea green tail and dark green hair, with eyes and brows outlined in dark green. This figure is naive indeed but is just the type of wood sculpture from which our modern sophisticates have derived inspiration.

133.   Mermaid

134. Devil Bootjack

135. Striding Man Doorstop

136. Goat

137.   Deer

138. Fireman

139. Kris Kringle

140. Poodle

141. Eagle

142. Cock

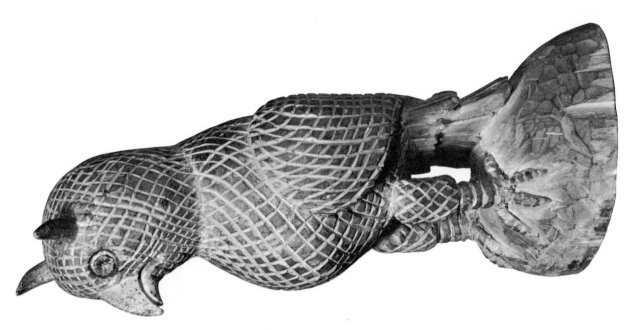

144. Owl

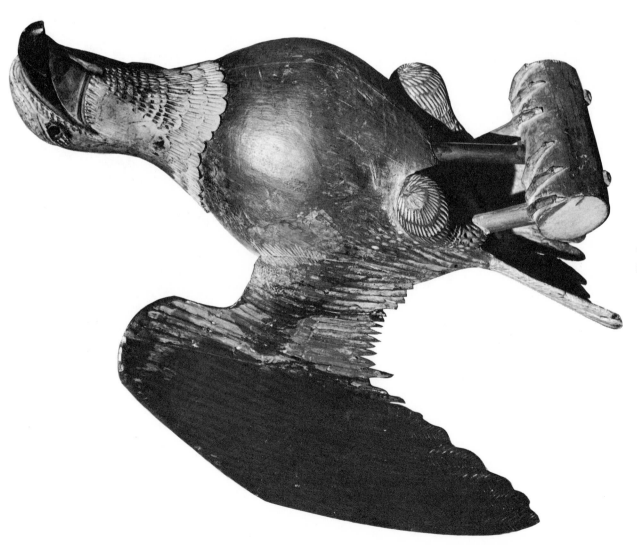

143. Eagle

145. Squirrel Bottle

146. Hitching-Post Head

147. Proposal

148.   Rooster

149. Sheep Pudding Mold

150. Cat Doorstop

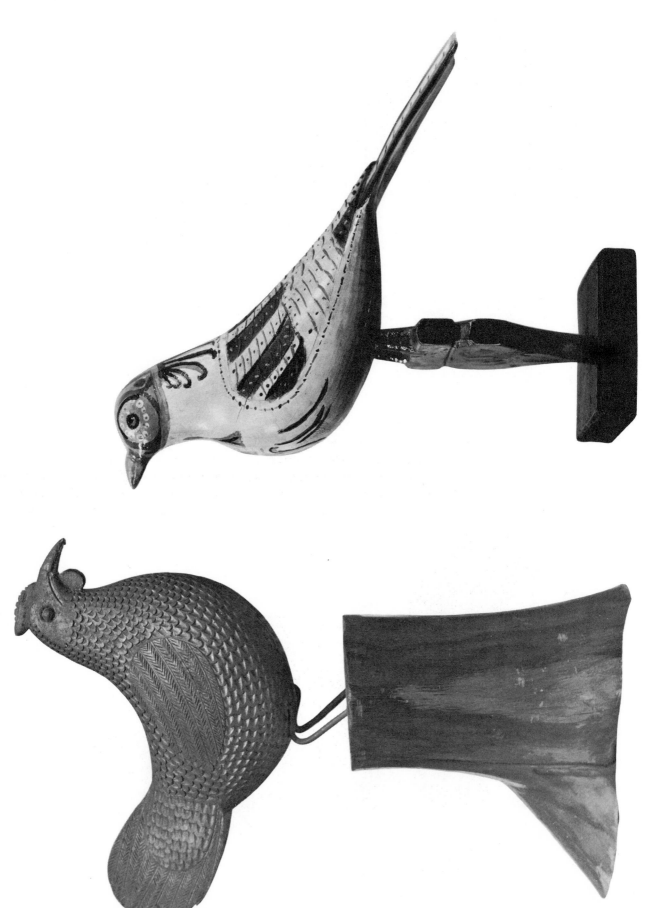

151. Little Wooden Hen

153.   Seated Figure of Liberty

(Reproduced in color on back cover)

154. William Pitt   155. Huntsman

156. George Washington

157.   Man on Horseback

158.   Bear Doorstop

159. Cake Board

160. Butter Mold

161.   Wedding Fable

162.   Deer Hunter

163.   The Plow

164.   Stiegel Stove-Plate

165. Horseman and Convicts

166. Gate

167. State of Maine Seal

168. Coat of Arms of Massachusetts

PORTRAITS

Portraits were painted in America during the seventeenth century, while native portrait sculpture originated in the early seventeen-hundreds. Not nearly as many examples of sculpture are to be found as of painting, but the early portraits of stone and wood are among the most interesting products of our folk art tradition. Some of the earliest portrait sculptures found in America were good, realistic pieces imported from England by wealthy families, and subsequently imitated by urban sculptors like William Rush of Philadelphia and later academicians. At the same time, however, a group of native stonecutters and ship carvers tried their hands at portraiture. Their technical training was simply that of well-grounded craftsmen, but their achievements surpassed those of the academic sculptors in originality and vigor.

The first native sculptors were the early New England stonecutters whose gravestone portraits we illustrate in Figs. 169–177. In 1927 Harriette M. Forbes published a scholarly book on these gravestones, including a detailed study of chronology, provenance, authorship, materials, techniques, subjects, and styles, some aspects of which are touched upon in this chapter.

American gravestones are recorded from 1653, and during the seventeenth century these were commonly ornamented with carved death's-heads, skeletons, cherubs, and mermaids. Not until the eighteenth century did portraiture appear, and gravestone portraits were not usual until the second half of the century. The tombstone portraits of Grindall Rawson by William Codner (1715), and of the Rev. Samuel Ruggles (1737) are exceptionally early (Figs. 170 & 174).

William Codner of Boston seems to have been one of the first to introduce the vogue for gravestone portraiture. In this he was followed by a sizeable number of Massachusetts stonecutters including Daniel Hastings of Newton and several members of the Park family of Groton, as well as one John Stevens of Rhode Island. Among the stones we illustrate, two of the Massachusetts examples may be definitely attributed. The fine portrait of John Holyoke (Fig. 171) was carved on a slab of slate by Daniel Hastings of Newton. Colonel Oliver Partridge of Hatfield (Fig. 177) was carved in white marble by his kinsman, Solomon Ashley of Deerfield. It is interesting to note that the majority of early likenesses on gravestones are found in country rather than city burying grounds.

The materials of the early gravestones were mostly native slate, marble, soapstone, and fieldstones of every variety, though some were made from slate which had been brought from England or Wales. The type of slate or stone had a good deal to do with the technique, slate lending itself to sharply incised contours and flat planes, marble and other stones to more rounded relief.

The gravestone portraits had evolved from the death's head and angel, which were quite generalized in most instances but appear portrait-like in some, and were intended to stand for, if not actually to resemble, the deceased at the Judgment Day. The representation of John Holyoke with wings is clearly a portrait developed from the conventionalized winged angels, which were abstract symbols for the dead in the earlier stones. The first portraits were frequently carved on the stone in combination with a skull, hourglass, scythe, or other symbol of the flight of time and the presence of death.

All varieties of portraits were executed, from the simple bust portrait in an oval frame to the full-length representation. One gravestone portrays a mother with an infant in her arms, standing in an arched doorway, another a Newburyport gentleman seemingly unaware of a skeleton holding a scythe, who approaches behind him and points an arrow at his back. Occasionally the portrait of the husband appears on the wife's grave, and vice versa.

Because they are always dated the early portrait gravestones provide valuable records of the appearance of the people and the dress of their day. We see specimens of all the individuals who made up eighteenth-century society—minister, soldier, schoolmaster, gentleman, housewife, child—accurately portrayed in the fashion then in vogue in that walk of life. The minister is seen in the burial ground today as his parishioners saw him every Sunday at church, in formal wig and devout expression. The fine lady may be observed wearing her best clothes and jewels, with hair carefully arranged.

The portraits vary greatly in the degree to which the sculptor individualized his subject. Although details of dress are factual, gravestone portraits even more than primitive painted portraits tended to generalize the appearance of the subject. The frank face of Polly Very of Salem (Fig. 173) is an unusually direct and individualized gravestone portrait of an engaging eighteenth-century wench. The early stonecutters most often created a timeless, eternal type of portraiture which was peculiarly appropriate for gravestone effigies. In these early likenesses, which have survived time and weather for generation upon generation, we see the very type of the pioneer New Englander, hardy and confident.

Each of the stonecutters had a personal style, which is generally more distinctly communicated in his portraiture than the individual facial characteristics of the subjects he portrayed. Solomon Ashley of Deerfield, who executed the likeness of Colonel Oliver Partridge (Fig. 177), developed a stylized portrait formula that is unmistakable. Another of his gravestones, for a Mr. William Rubble buried in Pownal, Vermont, shows such identical facial characteristics that, if there had been no inscription, and one was not aware of the attitude of the early stonecutter, one would assume the two men to have been twins.

The gravestone for the Holmes children (Fig. 176) is an extraordinary example of the conventionalized style of tombstone portraiture. The four profiles, almost identical, form a hieratic repeat design which calls to mind an Egyptian relief. Separated by the symbolic family tree with four broken branches, the "Four Lovely and promising Sons" are immobilized in stone. There is no parallel in any other American portraiture for such radically formalized design.

After looking at the gravestone effigies it is entertaining to read some of the gravestone epitaphs that were their literary counterpart. The gravestone portraits deserve a high place in our record of folk sculpture and some of the epitaphs have been repeated until they are now part and parcel of our folklore. The same spare Yankee vigor characterizes the pioneer folk carvings and the homely folklore inscriptions on the tombstones. As it seems likely that the stonecutters in some cases at least originated as well as lettered the inscriptions for the gravestones, it seems worth quoting a few typical examples. These, it should be noted, are somewhat later than the gravestone portraits we have reproduced.

The stone of a Cape Cod fisherman, Captain Thomas Coffin, succinctly describes his life and death:

> He has finished catching cod
> And gone to meet his God.

A brisk, prosaic epitaph on a stone at Oxford, New Hampshire, reads:

> To all my friends I bid adieu,
> A more sudden death you never knew.
> As I was leading the old mare to drink
> She kicked and killed me quicker'n a wink.

Grim verses describe with unsparing sharpness the fate of a young woman who died at Milford, Connecticut, in 1792:

> Molly, 'tho pleasant in her day,
> Was sudd'nly seized and sent away.
> How soon she's ripe, how soon she's rotten,
> Laid in the grave and soon forgott'n.

Like the carved portraits the verses are often crude, always direct. Here is one, showing, if nothing else, that no problem could faze the stonecutter, or the family of the deceased in thinking up an appropriate verse:

> Here lies John Auricular
> Who in the way of the Lord walked perpendicular.

An epitaph from a stone in Searsport, Maine, exemplifies the dry New England wit of the sort relished by simple country folk:

> Under the sod and under the trees
> Here lies the body of Solomon Pease
> The Pease are not here there's only the pod
> The Pease shelled out and went to God.

The last two we quote are untraced, but they are recorded by oral tradition and somehow have the ring of authenticity:

> Here lies the body of Sophronia Proctor
> Who had a cold, but wouldn't doctor.
> She couldn't stay, she had to go.
> Praise God from whom all blessings flow.

> Beneath this little mound of clay
> Lies Captain Ephraim Daniels,
> Who chose the dangerous month of May
> To change his winter flannels.

It is tempting to continue in this vein, but we had best return to a more serious discussion of portrait sculpture. We have touched on tombstone portraiture, which represents the one major field of folk carving in stone. The only free-standing portraits of any importance were carved of wood, and among these are some of the major products of American folk art. Before considering them we should mention the chalkware busts made by the Pennsylvania Germans, of which an example is illustrated (Fig. 182), and the portrait medallions which, like the busts, were made in molds of plaster of Paris and painted in the bright colors typical of Pennsylvania chalk. Political and military personages were the most common subjects for the busts, and the most popular portrait medallions seem to have been profiled likenesses of Andrew Jackson and his wife. These portraits of national heroes were made in quantity and priced low for popular consumption.

Wax portraits represent another minor branch of portrait sculpture, but we have not illustrated any of these because it did not seem that they properly belonged in a study of folk art. The wax portraits, popular during the eighteenth and early nineteenth centuries, were executed with finished, illusionistic modeling; and it is significant that the best-known American wax portrait artist, Patience Wright, won acclaim in England and executed a good deal of her work there. The two next most famous wax portraitists, John Christian Rauscher and Robert Ball Hughes, were natives of Germany and England respectively. Rauscher worked in an accomplished, academic German style, and Hughes won awards at the Royal Academy in London.

The cast iron statues of George and Martha Washington, manufactured by the Mott Iron Works for garden ornaments in the second half of the nineteenth century, were conventionally designed and of slight significance as folk portraiture.

It is among the simple woodcarved portraits, which developed Yankee whittling to a fine art, that we find a continuation of the vigorous, homely style that distinguishes the eighteenth-century tombstones. The earlier work of Rush and, with some exceptions, of McIntire is, as we have remarked, outside the folk art pale. Rush's portraiture was consistently based on the academic English style. McIntire's portraits, well exemplified by a bust of Governor Winthrop in the American Antiquarian Society and a medallion portrait of Washington in the Essex Institute, are less academic than Rush's work, but are not quite on the folk art level.

We have already mentioned and reproduced carved portraits from almost all the fields of folk sculpture which we have considered. Two of the carved portraits here reproduced (Figs. 178 & 180) could, on the other hand, have been illustrated in connection with decorative sculpture, and one (Fig. 179) was very possibly designed for some sort of ship decoration. In our discussion, therefore, we shall review woodcarved portraits, in general, and shall refer to reproductions that occur in this and the other chapters.

We have illustrated a number of figurehead portraits—Andrew Jackson from the warship *Constitution,* and Alice Knowles and George Skolfield and General Porter, from the ships that bore their names (Figs. 1, 12, 17, 18). It is likely that the lady with the umbrella (Fig. 10), which was found in Nantucket, was a whale ship's portrait figurehead. The stern carving from a whaling brig portraying one Eunice Adams (Fig. 22) was discussed. It seems probable that the thoughtful gentleman carved in relief for the sternpiece of some unidentified vessel (Fig. 23) was a portrait of the captain as he sat in his cabin, surrounded by the appurtenances of his calling.

There were an almost infinite number of cigar-store portraits of famous persons. The New-York Historical Society owns a figure of Osceola the Indian, and the Indian shown in Fig. 58 is an identified chief. The Rev. Campbell (Fig. 75), though used at one time as a cigar-store figure, was ordered and executed solely as a portrait. Harry Howard, the fire chief (Fig. 74), was a dramatically posed portrait used to ornament a fire house. "Col. Sellers" (Fig. 68) attracted attention to his apothecary shop. We have also mentioned the likenesses of Jenny Lind that were made both for cigar stores and circus wagons.

Even in the category of toys we might identify some portrait carvings, for dolls are said occasionally to have been carved with the features of their young mistresses. The policeman (Fig. 101) might well have been designed to look like some dignified officer personally known to the carver.

Among the decorative pieces the carving of George Washington was a true-to-life portrait even though based on earlier prints or paintings. The figures of famous men carved by or in the shop of Joseph Wilson for the Timothy Dexter estate made up a portrait gallery in wood that has never been rivalled, and it is a great pity that William Pitt (Fig. 154) must represent them all as the sole survivor.

The bust of Milton by Simeon Skillin, whom we have mentioned as among the ablest of the early carvers, tops the pediment of a secretary which he made for Moses Brown (Fig. 180). Skillin was not only a ship carver but a "house carver and furniture maker" as well. Windsor chairs were advertised at the Messrs. Skillin's shop in Boston and a number of important pieces of eighteenth-century furniture have been identified as Simeon's work, for the figures with which he ornamented them are characteristic of his bold style. The little figure reproduced is fairly bursting with vitality and good humor, and it seems as if Skillin must have used some contemporary face for the model of his laurel-wreathed bard, who has a refreshingly lively, everyday look.

One Alexander Ames, who worked in the neighborhood of Buffalo, New York, about 1850, seems to have specialized in carved bust portraits of children. These carvings are quite unique in the field of folk portraiture and are very similar in spirit to the best of the primitive paintings of children. Among his known portraits are the head of a boy in the New York State Historical Association at Cooperstown and portraits of three sisters, one privately owned (Fig. 181) and two in the collections of the Albright Art Gallery in Buffalo and the museum at Fitchburg, Massachusetts.

The portrait bust of General McClellan (Fig. 179), which was carved in 1862 and was found in Thomaston, Maine, is of pine painted buff, white and gold. It seems most likely, judging from its style, that this portrait, if not actually made to ornament some ship, was executed by a Maine ship carver. The rigid pose of the figure contrasts interestingly with the rich curves of the foliated scroll which frames the portrait. The face is quite expressionless, exemplifying a disciplined kind of craft carving which explores the planes and contours of the wood rather than the subtleties of personality.

The unidentified woman (Fig. 178) is as abstract and immobile a portrait as General McClellan. She is seated in a simple country chair, and looks as if she might have been in the act of winding yarn or some such housewifely occupation. The prime interest of this figure lies, however, in the realm of pure carved design.

It is the balanced contours of the figure, the rhythmic repeats of the tiered skirt and the linear zig-zag and dotted decoration of the dress that catch and hold our eye. Even the head resolves itself into a pattern in which the exactly oval eyes and mouth are separated by a triangle of nose, the whole outlined by symmetrical scallops of hair.

The portrait of Henry Ward Beecher (Fig. 183) is said to have been carved about 1850 by a farmer named Corbin at Centerville, Indiana, during a visit which Beecher paid to Corbin's home. Through the most elementary means the humble carver transformed a log of wood into a vital figure which communicates the inspiration of a man of God. The body enclosed in a shell-like coat serves as a plain, organic base for the dramatically uplifted head; and our attention focuses on the squarely modeled face and tiny, tense hands that clutch and support a heavy Bible. The absolute simplicity of contour and plastic expressiveness make this homely carving a masterpiece of the highest order. It is a specific interpretation of a pioneer American life; and it is also sculpture reduced to its universal common denominator.

169.   Rev. William Whitwell

170.   Grindall Rawson

171.   John Holyoke

172.   Charles Brigham

173.   Polly Very

174.   Rev. Samuel Ruggles

175. Mrs. Betheam Moseley

This Monument is erected to the Memory of Four Lovely and promiſing Sons of Mr. Appleton & Mrs. Lydia Holmes.

Appleton died Feb. 24th AD 1795 in the 9th Year of his Age~

Burridg died Dec. 20th AD 1794 in the 12th Year of his Age~

Ozias died Feb. 23d AD 1795 in the 7th Year of his Age.

Calvin died Feb. 25th AD 1795 in the 12th Year of his Age~

176. Holmes Children

177. Col. Oliver Partridge

178. Seated Woman

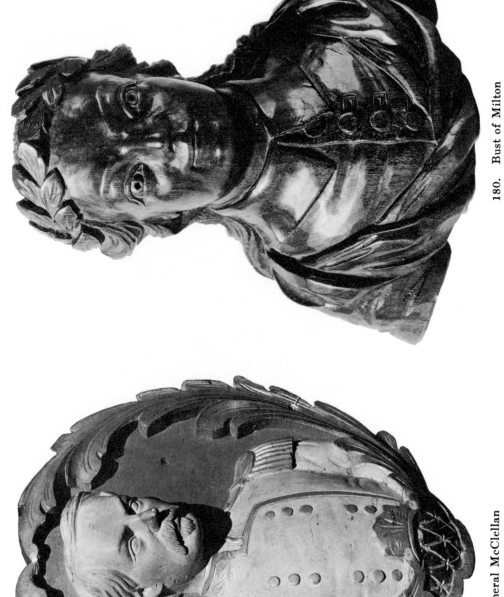

180.   Bust of Milton

179.   General McClellan

182. Military Gentleman

181. Head of Child

183. Henry Ward Beecher

BIBLIOGRAPHY

BACKGROUND

Adams, J. T., *Provincial Society*, Macmillan, N. Y., 1927.

Beard, C. A. & M. R., "Provincial America," v. 1, chap. 1 in *The Rise of American Civilization*, Macmillan, N. Y., 1930.

Botkin, B. A., ed., *A Treasury of American Folklore*, Crown, N. Y., 1944.

Dow, G. F., *The Arts & Crafts in New England 1704–1775, Gleanings from Boston Newspapers*, Wayside Press, Topsfield, Mass., 1927.

Dunlap, William, *A History of the Rise and Progress of the Arts of Design in the United States*, 1834. Dover reprint, 1969.

Fish, C. R., *The Rise of the Common Man, 1830–1850*, Macmillan, N. Y., 1927.

Flexner, J. T., *American Painting, First Flowers of Our Wilderness*, Houghton Mifflin, Boston, 1947. Dover reprint, 1969.

Lipman, Jean, *American Primitive Painting*, Oxford, 1942. Dover reprint, 1972.

Weygandt, Cornelius, *The Dutch Country*, Appleton-Century, N. Y., 1939.

Weygandt, Cornelius, *The Red Hills*, University of Pennsylvania Press, Phila., 1929.

Wright, Richardson, *Hawkers and Walkers in Early America*, Lippincott, Phila., 1927.

GENERAL

Albright Art Gallery, Catalogue, *Centennial Exhibition—American Folk Art*, Buffalo, July 1-Aug. 1, 1932.

Anon., "The Eagle in Americana," *Antiques*, XLIV (July 1943), 34-35.

Anon., *Pennsylvania German Arts and Crafts* (A Picture Book), Metropolitan Museum of Art, N. Y., 1942.

Anon., "Some Carved Figures by Samuel McIntire," *Bulletin of the Metropolitan Museum of Art*, XVIII (Aug. 1923), 194-95.

Banks, M. A., "American Folk Art—Three Recent Acquisitions," *Bulletin of the Museum of Art Rhode Island School of Design*, XXVIII (Nov. 1940), 51-54.

Born, Wolfgang, "American Primitives: In Their Relation to Europe and the Orient," *Antiques*, LII (Sept. 1947), 180-82.

Branscombe, Henry, "Early American Wood Sculpture," *International Studio*, LXXXVIII (Oct. 1927), 61-64.

Burroughs, P. H., *Southern Antiques*, Garret & Massie, Richmond, Va., 1931.

Cahill, Holger, "American Folk Art," *American Mercury*, XXIV (Sept. 1931), 39-46.

Cahill, Holger, "Folk Art—Its Place in the American Tradition," *Parnassus*, IV (Mar. 1932), 1-4.

(Cahill, Holger), Metropolitan Museum of Art, Catalogue, *Emblems of Unity and Freedom* (Index of American Design), N. Y., (1942).

(Cahill, Holger), Museum of Modern Art, Catalogue, *American Folk Art*, N. Y., 1932.

(Cahill, Holger & Robinson, E. B.), Newark Museum, Catalogue, *American Folk Sculpture*, Newark, N. J., 1931.

Christensen, E. O., "American Popular Art as Recorded in the Index of American Design," *Art in America*, XXXV (July 1947), 199-208.

Cooper, Nancy, "Wooden Eagles of New England Coast Towns," *House Beautiful*, LXII (Nov. 1927), 552, 606.

Cousins, Frank & Riley, P. M., *The Wood-carver of Salem* (Samuel McIntire), Little Brown, Boston, 1916.

Detroit Society of Arts and Crafts, Catalogue, *American Folk Art, Painting and Sculpture*, Feb. 22-Mar. 18, 1932.

Downs, Joseph, *The House of the Miller at Milbach—The Architecture, Arts and Crafts of the Pennsylvania Germans,* Pennsylvania Museum of Art, 1929.

Downtown Gallery, Catalogue, *American Birds in Sculpture,* N. Y., Jan. 30-Feb. 15, 1936.

Downtown Gallery, Catalogue, *American Folk Art Sculpture—Index of Design,* N. Y., Sept. 28-Oct. 9, 1937.

Downtown Gallery, Catalogue, *Loan Exhibition,* N. Y., Oct.-Nov., 1945.

Downtown Gallery, Catalogue, *Masterpieces in American Folk Art,* N. Y., Feb.-Mar., 1941.

Drepperd, C. W., *American Pioneer Arts & Artists,* Pond-Ekberg, Springfield, Mass., 1942.

Dyer, W. A., *Early American Craftsmen,* Century, N. Y., 1915.

Eberlein, H. D. & McClure, Abbott, *The Practical Book of American Antiques* (chap. XIV), Lippincott, Phila., 1927.

Eberlein, H. D. & McClure, Abbott, *The Practical Book of Early American Arts and Crafts* (chaps. IV & XIV), Lippincott, Phila., 1916.

Edgerton Giles, "Birds in Decoration," *Arts and Decoration,* XLIV (May 1936), 28-29.

Everhart Museum, Catalogue, *Early American Folk Art,* Scranton, Pa., n.d.

Gardner, A. T., *Yankee Stonecutters,* Columbia University Press, N. Y., 1945.

(Halpert, E. G.), Colonial Williamsburg, Inc., Catalogue, *American Folk Art,* Williamsburg, Va., 1940.

Kauffman, Henry, *Pennsylvania Dutch American Folk Art,* 1946. Dover reprint, 1964.

Keyes, H. E., "Title-Hunting Americana," *Antiques,* XXIII (Feb. 1933), 59-61.

Lichten, Frances, *Folk Art of Rural Pennsylvania,* Scribner's, N. Y., 1946.

Lipman, Jean, "The Study of Folk Art," *Art in America,* XXIII (Oct. 1945), 245-54.

Marceau, Henri, *William Rush,* Pennsylvania Museum of Art, Phila., 1937.

Pease, Z. W., *A Visit to the Museum of the Old Dartmouth Historical Society,* Old Dartmouth Historical Society, New Bedford, Mass., 1947 (4th ed.)

Robacker, E. F., *Pennsylvania Dutch Stuff,* University of Pennsylvania Press, Phila., 1944.

Swan, M. M., "Boston's Carvers and Joiners," *Antiques,* LIII (March 1948), 198-201.

SHIP FIGUREHEADS AND ORNAMENTS

Anon., "The Figurehead and its Story," *Scientific American,* CI (Aug. 7, 1909), 92-93, 101-03.

Anon., *Figureheads and Ship Decorations,* 12 vol. scrapbook, gift of E. A. McCann, 1933 (New York Public Library).

Brown, A. C., "Paddle Box Decorations of American Sound Steamboats," reprinted from *American Neptune,* III (no. 1, 1943), Mariners' Museum, Newport News, Va.

Clark, A. H., *The Clipper Ship Era,* Putnam's, N. Y., 1910.

Conrad, Joseph, "Smile of Fortune" in *Twixt Land and Sea,* Doubleday Page, N. Y., 1912.

Gould, G. G., "Nadelman Ship Figureheads," *International Studio,* XCIV (Sept. 1929), 51-53.

Hawthorne, Nathaniel, "Drowne's Wooden Image" in *Mosses from an Old Manse,* Houghton Mifflin, Boston, 1882.

Leslie, R. C., *Old Sea Wings, Ways and Words, in the Days of Oak and Hemp* (chaps. X & XI), Chapman Hall, London, 1890.

Laughton, L. G. C., *Old Ship Figureheads and Sterns,* Halton & Smith, London, 1925.

Longfellow, H. W., "The Building of the Ship," *The Complete Poetical Works of Henry Wadsworth Longfellow,* Houghton Mifflin, Boston, 1893.

Pinckney, P. A., *American Figureheads and Their Carvers,* Norton, N. Y., 1940.

Rogers, C. N., "Ship Figureheads, Selections from the Collection of the Mariners' Museum," reprinted from *Shipyard Bulletin,* XI (Feb. 1946), Newport News Shipbuilding and Dry Dock Co., Newport News, Va.

Swan, M. M., "Ship Carvers of Newburyport," *Antiques,* XLVIII (Aug. 1945), 78-81.

Tucker, H. R., "Ship Figureheads," *North Shore Breeze,* XII (Mar. 14, 1924), 1, 31.

Watson, E. S. & Hayward, Victoria, "Figureheads of the Old Square-riggers," *Century,* XCII (Aug. 1916), 566-73.

Zabriskie, G. A., "Ship Figureheads in and about New York," *New-York Historical Society Quarterly Bulletin,* XXX (Jan. 1946), 5-16.

WEATHERVANES

Allen, E. B., "Old American Weather Vanes," *International Studio,* LXXX (Mar. 1925), 450-53.

Anon., "And Joy, a Vane that Veers," *Antiques,* XVIII (Dec. 1930), 482.

Anon., "The Cover," *Antiques,* XXVIII (Oct. 1935), cover, 139.

Anon., "Lo, the Lofty Indian," *Antiques,* XXIX (Jan. 1936), 8-9.

Anon., "Running Fireman," *Antiques,* XLVIII (July 1945), 29.

Barr, A. H., *Picasso: Fifty Years of His Art,* Museum of Modern Art, N. Y., 1946 (quote re cock weathervanes).

Cushing, L. W., Catalogue of Weather Vanes Manufactured by L. W. Cushing and Sons, Waltham, Mass., 1883.

Downtown Gallery, Catalogue, *Exhibition of Early American Sculpture—Weathervanes,* N. Y., Sept. 16-Oct. 11, 1941.

Fiske, J. W., *Illustrated Catalogue and Price List of Copper Weather Vanes and Finials,* Barclay St. & Park Place, N. Y., n.d. (about 1890).

Halpert, E. G., "A Native American Art," *House & Garden,* LVXXX (Oct. 1941), 51, 86-87.

Harris & Co., *Boston Copper Weather Vanes,* 54 Bromfield St., Boston, 1879.

Wellman, Rita, "American Weathervanes," *House Beautiful,* LXXIV (Jan. 1939), 50-54, 69.

Whipple, J. R., "Old New England Weather Vanes," *Old-Time New England,* XXXI (Oct. 1940), 45-56.

CIGAR-STORE FIGURES AND OTHER TRADE SIGNS

Anon., *American Fire Marks. The Insurance Company of North America Collection.* Insurance Co. of North America, Phila., 1933.

Apperson, G. L., *The Social History of Smoking* (chap. 15), Putnam, N. Y., 1916.

Beebe, Lucius, *Mixed Train Daily—A Book of Short-line Railroads,* Dutton, N. Y., 1947.

Beebe, Lucius, "Railroad Art," *Antiques,* LII (Sept. 1947), 172-73.

Dickens, Charles, *Dombey and Son,* Crowell & Co., N. Y., n.d. (quote re trade sign figure).

Gillingham, H. E., *American Fire-marks,* privately printed, Phila., 1914.

Gillingham, H. E. "The Fascinating Fire-mark," *Antiques,* IV (Dec. 1923), 277-80.

Jessup, L. F., "The Tobacconists' Tribe of Treen," *Antiques,* XVIII (Sept. 1930), 232-35.

Lipman, Jean, "Two Nautical Shop Signs," *American Antiques Journal,* II (Jan. 1947), 14-15.

McCosker, M. J., *The Historical Collection of the Insurance Company of North America,* privately printed, Phila., 1945.

Morrison, J. L., "Passing of the Wooden Indian," *Scribner's Magazine,* LXXXIV (Oct. 1928), 393-405.

Sanborn, Kate, *Hunting Indians in a Taxi-cab,* Gorham Press, Boston, 1911.

Shaw, C. G., "My Little Indians," *House & Garden,* LXXXXIII (May 1948), 134, 186.

Turner, T. G., "Sentimental Hunks of Wood," *Los Angeles Times* (Sunday Magazine), Mar. 17, 1940, 3-4, 10.

Twain, Mark & Warner, C. D., *The Gilded Age,* Harper, N. Y., n.d. (quote re Col. Sellers).

Weitenkampf, F. W., "Lo, the Wooden Indian: The Art of Making Cigar-shop Signs," *New York Times,* Aug. 3, 1890, p. 13, col. 1.
Weitenkampf, F. W., *Manhattan Kaleidoscope,* Scribner's, N. Y., 1947.

CIRCUS AND CARROUSEL CARVINGS

Anon., "The Cover," *Antiques,* XLIV (July 1943), cover, 9, 33.
Howe, F. T., "Carved Wood Circus-wagon Figures," *Antiques,* LII (Aug. 1947), 120-21.
Peters, H. T., "The Greatest Show on Earth," *Antiques,* XXXVIII (July 1940), 15-17.
Werner, M. R., *Barnum,* Harcourt Brace, N. Y., 1923.
Whitehill, V. N., "American Circus Carving," *Magazine of Art,* XXXVI (May 1943), 172-75.

TOYS

Anon., "18th Century American Toy," *American Collector,* XVI (Dec. 1947), cover.
Anon., "Primitive Invasion," *Antiques,* XX (July 1931), 13.
Carrick, A. V. L., "Playthings of the Past," *Antiques,* I (Jan. 1922), 10-16.
Downtown Gallery, Catalogue, *Children in American Folk Art,* N. Y., Apr. 13-May 1, 1937.
Flower, M. E., "Schimmel the Woodcarver," *Antiques,* XLIV (Oct. 1943), 164-66.
Freeman, Ruth & Larry, *Cavalcade of Toys,* Century House, N. Y., 1942.
Hertz, L. H., *The Handbook of Old American Toys,* Mark Haber & Co., Wethersfield, Conn., 1947.
Holme, C. G., ed., *Children's Toys of Yesterday,* Studio Publications, N. Y., 1932.
Jackson, Mrs. F. N., *Toys of Other Days,* Scribner's, N. Y., 1908.
Johl, J. P., *The Fascinating Story of Dolls,* H. L. Lindquist Publications, N. Y., 1911.
Johl, J. P., *More About Dolls,* H. L. Lindquist Publications, N. Y., 1946.
McKearin, H. A., "Schimmel, Carver of a Menagerie," *New York Sun,* Nov. 16, 1929, p. 35, col. 1.
Winchester, Alice, "Blow Birds," *Antiques,* XLVIII (July 1945), 28-29.

DECOYS

Abercrombie & Fitch Co., Catalogue, *American Wild Fowl Decoys,* N. Y., Oct. 1-8, 1932.
Anon., "Add Americana: The Decoy," *Fortune,* VI (Aug. 1932), 38-42.
Barber, Joel, *Wild Fowl Decoys,* Windward House, N. Y., 1934 (first ed. Derrydale Press, N.Y., 1932). Dover reprint, 1954.

SCULPTURE FOR HOUSE AND GARDEN

Allis, Mary, "The Last of the American Folk Arts" (Chalkware), *American Collector,* IX (Jan. 1941), 10-11, 14.
Anon., "Another Skillin Sculpture Identified," *Antiques,* XXVIII (Oct. 1935), 140.
Anon., "Lord Dexter of Newburyport: The Voice of the People," *Antiques,* III (Mar. 1923), 107-08.
E. A. B., "Cast Iron Stoves of the Pennsylvania Germans," *Bulletin of the Pennsylvania Museum,* X (Apr. 1915), 19-23.
Coatsworth, Elizabeth, *Maine Ways* (pp. 95-98 on Edbury Hatch), Macmillan, N. Y., 1947.
Daland, E. L., "Engraved Types of Scrimshaw," *Antiques,* XXVIII (Oct. 1935), 153-55.
Dexter, Timothy, *A Pickel for the Knowing Ones,* Blanchard & Sargent, New Hampshire, 1848 (first ed. 1802).

Dyer, W. A., "American Firebacks and Stove Plates," *Antiques,* XXV (Feb. 1934), 60-63.

Fackenthal, B. F., "Classification and Analysis of Stove Plates," *Bucks County Historical Society Papers,* VII (1917), 55-61.

Gould, G. G., "Eighteenth Century Cottage Ornaments," *House & Garden,* LVII (May 1930), 124, 142-48.

Gould, G. G., "Plaster Ornaments for Collectors," *House & Garden,* LVI (Aug. 1929), 84, 122.

Green, S. M., Manuscript on Edbury Hatch, to be published in the *Magazine of Art.*

Howells, J. M., *The Architectural Heritage of the Merrimack,* Architectural Book Publishing Co., N. Y., 1941.

Marquand, J. P., *Lord Timothy Dexter of Newburyport, Massachusetts,* Minton Balch, N. Y., 1925.

Mercer, H. C., *The Bible in Iron,* Bucks County Historical Society, Doylestown, Pa., 1941 (first ed. 1914).

Robacker, E. F., *Pennsylvania German Cooky Cutters and Cookies,* Kutztown Publishing Co. (Home Craft Course), Kutztown, Pa., 1946.

Smith, Chetwood, *Rogers Groups,* Goodspeed, Boston, 1934.

Stow, C. M., "A Portrait in Iron," *Antiquarian,* XIV (June 1930), 29-31.

PORTRAITS

Bolton, E. S., *American Wax Portraits,* Houghton Mifflin, Boston, 1929.

Forbes, H. M., "Early Portrait Sculpture in New England," *Old-Time New England,* XVIII (Apr. 1929), 159-73.

Forbes, H. M., *Gravestones of Early New England and the Men who Made Them, 1653-1800,* Houghton Mifflin, Boston, 1927.

Mitchell, E. V., *It's an Old New England Custom* (chap. X), Vanguard Press, N. Y., 1946.

Taylor, E. A. O'D., "The Slate Gravestones of New England," *Old-Time New England,* XV (Oct. 1924), 58-67.